Endangered
Animals

VOLUME 7

Murrelet, Japanese – **Pupfish,** Devil's Hole

GROLIER
EDUCATIONAL

Published 2002 by Grolier Educational, Danbury, CT 06816

This edition published exclusively for the school and library market

Produced by Andromeda Oxford Limited
11–13 The Vineyard, Abingdon,
Oxon OX14 3PX, U.K.
www.andromeda.co.uk

Principal Contributors: *Amy-Jane Beer, Andrew Campbell, Robert and Valerie Davies, John Dawes, Jonathan Elphick, Tim Halliday, Pat Morris. Further contributions by David Capper and John Woodward*

Project Director: *Graham Bateman*
Managing Editors: *Shaun Barrington, Jo Newson*
Editor: *Penelope Mathias*
Art Editor and Designer: *Steve McCurdy*
Cartographic Editor: *Tim Williams*
Editorial Assistant: *Marian Dreier*
Picture Manager: *Claire Turner*
Production: *Clive Sparling*
Indexers: *Indexing Specialists, Hove, East Sussex*

Reproduction by A. T. Color, Milan
Printing by H & Y Printing Ltd., Hong Kong

Set ISBN 0-7172-5584-0

Library of Congress Cataloging-in-Publication Data

Endangered animals.
        p. cm.
        Contents: v. 1. What is an endangered animal? -- v. 2. Addax -
    blackbuck -- v. 3. Boa, Jamaican - danio, barred -- v. 4. Darter,
    Watercress - frog, gastric brooding -- v. 5. Frog, green and golden bell -
    kestrel, lesser -- v. 6. Kestrel, Mauritius - Mulgara -- v. 7. Murrelet,
    Japanese - Pupfish, Devil's Hole -- v. 8. Pygmy-possum, mountain - Siskin, red -- v.
    9. Skink, pygmy blue-tongued - tragopan, Temminck's -- v. 10. Tree-kangaroo,
    Goodfellow's - zebra, mountain.
        ISBN 0-7172-5584-0 (set : alk. paper) -- ISBN 0-7172-5585-9 (v. 1 : alk. paper) –
    ISBN 0-7172-5586-7 (v. 2 : alk. paper) -- ISBN 0-7172-5587-5 (v. 3 : alk. paper) –
    ISBN 0-7172-5588-3 (v. 4 : alk. paper) -- ISBN 0-7172-5589-1 (v. 5 : alk. paper) –
    ISBN 0-7172-5590-5 (v. 6 : alk. paper) -- ISBN 0-7172-5591-3 (v. 7 : alk. paper) –
    ISBN 0-7172-5592-1 (v. 8 : alk. paper) -- ISBN 0-7172-5593-X (v. 9 : alk. paper) –
    ISBN 0-7172-5594-8 (v. 10 : alk. paper)
        1. Endangered species--Juvenile literature. [1. Endangered species.] I. Grolier
    Educational (Firm)

    QL83 .E54 2001
    333.95'42--dc21

                                                                    00-069134

NA

Contents

About This Set

Endangered Animals is a 10-volume set that highlights and explains the threats to animal species across the world. Habitat loss is one major threat; another is the introduction of species into areas where they do not normally live.

Examples of different animals facing a range of problems have been chosen to include all the major animal groups. Fish, reptiles, amphibians, and insects and invertebrates are included as well as mammals and birds. Some species may have very large populations, but they nevertheless face problems. Some are already extinct.

Volume 1—What Is an Endangered Animal?—explains how scientists classify animals, the reasons why they are endangered, and what conservationists are doing about it. Cross-references in the text (volume number followed by page number) show relevant pages in the set.

Volumes 2 to 10 contain individual species entries arranged in alphabetical order. Each entry is a double-page spread with a data panel summarizing key facts and a locator map showing its range.

Look for a particular species by its common name, listed in alphabetical order on the Contents page of each book. (Page references for both common and scientific names are in the full set index at the back of each book.) When you have found the species that interests you, you can find related entries by looking first in the data panel. If an animal listed under Related endangered species has an asterisk (*) next to its name, it has its own separate entry. You can also check the cross-references at the bottom of the left-hand page, which refer to entries in other volumes. (For example, "Finch, Gouldian **4:** 74" means that the two-page entry about the Gouldian finch starts on page 74 of Volume 4.) The cross-reference is usually made to an animal that is in the same genus or family as the species you are reading about; but a species may appear here because it is from the same part of the world or faces the same threats.

Each book ends with a glossary of terms, lists of useful publications and websites, and a full set index.

Murrelet, Japanese

Synthliboramphus wumizusume

Limited to a few traditional breeding grounds on a scattering of small Japanese islands and a handful of feeding areas off the coast, the Japanese murrelet faces a variety of threats, mainly caused by humans.

Short and stout, with stubby wings and a rakish black crest in the breeding season, the Japanese murrelet is one of the smallest of the auks, the group of seabirds that includes the puffins, murres, and razorbills. Often described as the northern equivalent of penguins, auks live mostly at sea, where they dive for small fish and other prey, pursuing them by "flying" underwater, using their wings as well as their feet for propulsion and steering. They come to land only to breed, choosing coastal sites that provide easy access to the water and safe refuges from predators. Such places are scarce, so favored sites attract dense colonies of breeding birds. Where a species has a small range, the entire world population may be concentrated on a few islands and remote headlands, making it vulnerable to local disasters. Such is the case with the Japanese murrelet—one of the rarest and most endangered of all auks.

Island Breeding Grounds

The murrelet breeds only on a scattering of rocky islands off the coasts of central and southern Japan, where originally there were no land predators at all. The birds pair for life; and when they return to their traditional breeding grounds in early spring, the pairs often reoccupy nesting holes and crevices that they have used before. They take turns incubating a clutch of two eggs, leaving and returning by night. Soon after the chicks hatch, they fly with them to the sea. There they travel across open water for hours on end to reach offshore feeding grounds. They do not return to land until the next breeding season.

At sea the murrelets congregate in places where converging, nutrient-rich ocean currents concentrate small prey such as krill (shrimplike marine crustaceans) and larval fish into swarms and shoals. They may commute more than 30 miles (50 km) from their nesting colonies to reach such places. Once the breeding season is over, many of them move north to exploit the rich waters southeast of Hokkaido, the northernmost of Japan's main islands.

DATA PANEL

Japanese murrelet

Synthliboramphus wumizusume

Family: Alcidae

World population: 5,000–6,000, possibly 10,000 birds

Distribution: Coasts and islands around Japan; possibly breeds in Russia, and there are single records for Taiwan and South Korea

Habitat: Feeds in the warm ocean currents flowing around Japan; breeds on small, uninhabited islands around central and southern Japan

Size: Length: 10 in (25 cm). Weight: 6 oz (170 g)

Form: A small, squat auk with a short neck, short wings, and short tail. Black head with (in summer only) black crest and white stripes extending from eyes to nape; black and blue-gray upperparts; dark-gray flanks; white underparts; short, thick, blue-gray bill; grayish-yellow legs and feet

Diet: Krill and other planktonic crustaceans, plus shrimp and small larval fish such as herring, smelt, and sandeels, caught by pursuit diving

Breeding: Pairs for life, nesting from mid-February to early May in pairs or small colonies, using rock crevices, hollows, and burrows. Two eggs are incubated for about 4.5–5 weeks by both parents. Chicks leave nest within 2 days of hatching and follow parents to sea, to be reared until fully grown at about 1 month old

Related endangered species: Many auks are threatened, including several in North Pacific: Craveri's murrelet (*Synthliboramphus craveri*) VU; Xantus's murrelet (*S. hypoleucus*) VU; marbled murrelet (*Brachyramphus marmoratus*) VU

Status: IUCN VU; not listed by CITES

RUSSIA
CHINA
NORTH KOREA
SOUTH KOREA
JAPAN

See also: Island Biogeography 1: 30; Pollution 1: 50; Introductions 1: 54; Auk, Great 2: 38

They feed only in shallow water over the continental shelf, which does not extend far off the Japanese coast, so for much of the time they stay within relatively small sea areas. Such concentration makes the population vulnerable to oil spills.

Threats from Predators and Fish Nets

The most direct threats to Japanese murrelet colonies come from the black rats probably accidentally introduced to their nesting islands by fishermen. These animals destroy nestlings and even adult birds, but their main targets are unattended eggs. They are joined in the feast by gulls and crows, attracted by fish discarded by sport anglers who land on the islands. Consequently only 38 percent of eggs laid result in viable chicks. Between them the rats and crows have destroyed entire breeding colonies on several islands. Of 10 colonies that flourished in the Izu Islands in the 1950s, seven have been wiped out, and another is on the verge of annihilation, mostly because of predators.

The murrelets have also suffered through competition with people. In recent years the small crustaceans and fish on which they feed have become a valuable human resource, and are scooped from the sea by the ton. Like auks all over the world, Japanese murrelets are finding it increasingly difficult to get sufficient quantities of food. Other fisheries make hunting not only fruitless but dangerous by littering the seas with deadly drift nets that trap the birds underwater so that they drown. It has been estimated that up to 10 percent of the murrelet breeding population is killed in this way each year. Others are poisoned by oil routinely

The Japanese murrelet
is threatened by disturbance of breeding sites, predation, and the activities of drift-net fisheries.

dumped in the sea by shipping, so they either die or fail to breed—and a major oil spill in the waters where they feed could destroy most of the Japanese murrelet population in a few days.

As a result of all these problems the population has declined to 10,000 at most, and probably to a lot fewer. Most of the colonies are still dwindling, and half the world population now nests on just one island, Biro-jima, off Kyushu. Here the nesting birds suffer particularly badly from harassment by crows. Murrelets are long-lived, slow-breeding birds, so they cannot exploit brief flushes of food to build up their numbers, and the only hope of arresting their decline is a permanent commitment to their conservation.

Saving the Japanese murrelet will involve eliminating all ground predators from the birds' breeding islands as well as restricting human access. The setting up of new reserves to add to those that are already National Wildlife Protection Areas is also planned. Other protective measures include working on ways to reduce the number of adult birds trapped in fishing nets. If its breeding colonies are made secure, the Japanese murrelet may still be able to hold its own.

Mussel, Freshwater

Margaritifera auricularia

About 10 species of freshwater mussels occur in Europe, and more are found in America. Generally they are inconspicuous members of the lake and riverbed animal communities, but two—in the genus Margaritifera—*have become famous for their pearls, and overcollection has endangered them.*

Freshwater mussels are bivalve mollusks: Their bodies are enclosed within two shells that are attached by a hinge. They have many structural features in common with their marine relatives the common mussel and the common oyster. The shells, technically known as valves, are secreted by the outer skin of the body that is called the mantle. The mantle and the shells cover the whole body and also enclose a space referred to as the mantle cavity. The shells and mantle cavity open along the underside of the animal as well as at the front and back.

Inside a Mussel Shell

Many of the important daily activities of the mussel—such as respiration, feeding, excretion, reproduction, and even activities related to locomotion—take place inside the mantle space. When the mussel is in its normal orientation, the hinge of the shells is on the upper side. Immediately below the hinge area, inside the shells, lies the main body. It includes the head, mouth, digestive tract, digestive organs, reproductive organs, and heart. Hanging down into the mantle cavity are two pairs of gills, one on the left side and one on the right. They run the whole length of the shells. Between each pair, in the middle, is a hydraulically operated foot, which is extended by blood pressure. The head is poorly developed in relation to the rest of the body, and it lacks complex receptor organs like eyes, but it has a pair of leaflike palps that have a sensory function and assist in the ingestion of food.

The shells can be closed tightly together by the contraction a pair of adductor muscles that run from one shell to the other. When the muscles contract and close the shells, they also compress a rubbery ligament, which is sandwiched between them near the hinge. The adductor muscles have special qualities that enable them to contract for long periods of time. When the muscles relax, the compressed, rubbery ligament forces the shells open like a spring.

Freshwater mussels mainly inhabit muds, sands, and gravels on the beds of rivers and lakes. They

DATA PANEL

Freshwater mussel (Spengler's freshwater mussel)

Margaritifera auricularia

Family: Margaritiferidae

World population: Unknown

Distribution: Europe, from Portugal east to the Czech Republic

Habitat: Freshwater rivers, streams, and lakes through which rivers flow

Size: Length: up to 5 in (12 cm)

Form: Typical mussel or clam shape; body enclosed in 2 shells

Diet: Plant plankton and detrital particles

Breeding: Larvae develop from fertilized eggs carried internally on the mussel's gills and are expelled when they have developed hooks;

they catch hold of the fins of passing fish and get carried around for about 2 weeks before they drop off and complete their development on the river or lake bed

Related endangered species: Freshwater pearl mussel (*Margaritifera margaritifera*) EN; Louisiana pearlshell (*M. hembeli*) CR; Alabama pearlshell (*M. marrianae*) EN

Status: IUCN CR; not listed by CITES

See also: Categories of Threat **1:** 14; Luxury Products **1:** 46; Clam, Giant **3:** 50

normally live with
part of their bodies
buried, and they achieve
this using the foot. The foot is inflated with blood and
extends down between the shells into the substratum.
Its tip then widens and forms an anchor in the
sediment. By using the foot, the freshwater mussel
can stay in the substratum or move itself slowly along,
plowing through the sediment with a jerky movement.

The gills are major organs that are also found
inside the mantle cavity. They are made up of vertically
arranged filaments covered in fine, beating threads
called cilia that are invisible to the naked eye. The
beating cilia create a current so that water is drawn in
at the rear between the shells and passed across the
surface of the gills. Here oxygen is absorbed into the
body from the water, and carbon dioxide is passed out
into the water. As is so often the case in the animal
kingdom, a ciliated respiratory stream of water is also
used for feeding, and the gills serve a second function
as sieves to strain suitable particles of food from the
water currents.

Freshwater mussels *are able to anchor themselves to a
river or lake bed by means of a hydraulically operated foot.
The foot also allows jerky movement through the sediment.*

Overcollection for Pearls

Bivalve mollusks like oysters and mussels are well
known for the way in which they respond to irritants
from foreign bodies or parasites inside the shell. A
coating of nacre, the pearly innermost layer of the
bivalve shell, is deposited around the intrusion, and as
it is secreted, a pearl grows. *Margaritifera auricularia*
and its close relative *Margaritifera margaritifera* are
known for their ability to form pearls, which although
being less lustrous than the traditional oyster pearls,
are still desirable. Overcollection of freshwater mussels
in search of pearls has caused a serious reduction in
their populations. In fact, numbers of *margaritifera
auricularia* have been so depleted that the IUCN has
classified the species as Critically Endangered.

Nemertine, Rodrigues

Geonemertes rodericana

The Rodrigues nemertine was discovered on the island of Rodrigues (Rodriguez) in the Indian Ocean in 1874. It is now at risk from habitat destruction.

Very few people will have even heard of nemertine worms, let alone seen one. The common name for the group, ribbon worms, at least gives some indication of what these animals look like. Nemertine worms have relatively long, narrow, flattened bodies, which can be shortened by contraction of the muscles that run the length of the animal and lengthened by muscles that circle the body. The body is not divided up into segments, and there are consequently no distinct rings along the worm as in earthworms, for example.

The head is not very clearly defined, but it bears a mouth, a pair of sensory pits, and groups of simple eyes that can be made out with the aid of a microscope. Internally the gut passes from the mouth at the front to the anus at the rear of the body. There is a simple blood vascular (circulation) system, but the worms do not have a heart, so blood is squeezed through the body by contraction of muscles.

Nemertine worms are mainly marine and are found on the seashore or the seabed, living under rocks or buried in sand and mud. However, a few species have ventured away from salt water, living at the top of the shore in damp soil and among vegetation, and even in trees.

One structure sets the nemertines apart from other worms: the special fluid-filled chamber known as the rhynchocoel. The long proboscis, which can be extended from the head, is normally held retracted inside the body in the space within the rhynchocoel. The proboscis is used for capturing prey and for defense in many species. In the Rodrigues nemertine the proboscis is very long, and the rhynchocoel stretches almost the full length of the animal.

The Rodrigues nemertine is terrestrial, and many of the differences between it and its marine relatives relate to the difficulties of movement and maintaining its body fluids when living on land. One adaptation for terrestrial life in the Rodrigues worm is the use of the proboscis as an additional locomotory organ. The whole animal can be stretched out with the proboscis

COMOROS

MADAGASCAR

MAURITIUS Rodrigues

Réunion
(France)

DATA PANEL

Rodrigues nemertine

(Rodriguez nemertine)

Geonemertes rodericana

Family: Prosorhoehmidae

World population: Unknown

Distribution: Rodrigues (Rodriguez) Island and Mauritius, Indian Ocean

Habitat: Damp soil and damp vegetation

Size: Length: variable according to degree of extension, often about 4 in (10 cm)

Form: Flattened, ribbonlike worm with protrusable (extendable) proboscis (feeding appendage) at the front

Diet: Small invertebrate animals

Breeding: Adults are hermaphrodite (have both male and female reproductive organs); eggs hatch within the parent's body, and young worms are delivered

Related endangered species: Probably several on isolated island sites

Status: IUCN DD; not listed by CITES

See also: Categories of Threat **1:** 14; What Is an Invertebrate? **1:** 80; Leech, Medicinal **6:** 20

The **Rodrigues nemertine** *was described by the naturalist Gulliver in 1874, who depicted it as green with a narrow white streak (left). Ribbon worms such as* Tubulanus superbus *(below) can stretch their bodies to several times their resting length.*

extended in front. The tip can then attach to the soil, and the animal can contract both body and proboscis, thus rapidly heaving itself forward. The large rhynchocoel also plays a useful role in storing body fluids in the Rodrigues nemertine, and the excretory system functions particularly to regulate the water content of the animal; with its soft body, desiccation (drying out) is a constant risk.

One could argue that the Rodrigues nemertine is on the cutting edge of nemertine evolution, trying every possible means of expanding into new habitats. However, the worm lacks the physiological resources to overcome the hazards of desiccation that affect many terrestrial habitats.

Under Threat

Some 11 species of *Geonemertes* are recognized, and they all have limited natural distributions; about nine are restricted to oceanic islands. In such circumstances their gene pool is not reinforced by immigration from outside, and they become vulnerable to local environmental changes. However, accidental distribution by people—probably by the horticultural trade—is common in the case of *Geonemertes* worms.

The Rodrigues nemertine was first reported in 1874, at which time the naturalist Gulliver found them to be "tolerably abundant." Specimens were brought back from another expedition in 1919. In 1993 an expedition found many nemertine worms, but none resembling Gulliver's description. They also found that most of the existing woodland on the island consists of introduced species, which have probably damaged the natural habitat of the Rodrigues nemertine.

The Rodrigues nemertine is classified by the IUCN as Data Deficient, but it could soon become Vulnerable as a result of environmental disturbances. Introducing "foreign" competitor species may also be as much of a threat as destroying existing habitat.

Nene

Branta sandvicensis

Unique to the Hawaiian Islands, the nene was driven to the verge of extinction by the destruction of its wild habitats and the introduction of predators. By 1950 there were only about 30 left on Hawaii, but captive breeding has helped, and the nene may soon be thriving again in the wild.

The volcanic Hawaiian Islands were once home to a unique variety of birdlife, including at least 11 species of waterfowl found nowhere else in the world. Perfectly adapted for life on the islands, where the only native predators were birds of prey, several of the geese and ducks were flightless. When the Polynesians arrived about 1,600 years ago, they were sitting targets, and most are now extinct. Only three of the 11 now survive, including the one big goose that was able to fly: the nene.

Also known as the Hawaiian goose, the nene is named for its high, nasal, two-note "né-né" call. Although it can fly, it has quite short wings—too short for a long migration. Fossil evidence shows that it once occurred throughout the Hawaiian chain. To make up for its short wings, it has unusually long legs, with big, strong feet. Since there is little wetland on the islands, it has little webbing between its toes, which are padded to help it scramble over the rocky lava flows that spill down the flanks of the island volcanoes.

Drinking water is hard to find on the islands, so the essentially vegetarian nene seeks out moisture-rich plants for food. In season it plucks berries from the bushes between the lava flows, making the most of its long legs to reach up into the foliage.

Hunted Out

The Polynesian settlers brought their pigs, dogs, and—accidentally—the Polynesian rat. They all played havoc with the ground-nesting nene. People also burned off the lowland scrub to create pasture, destroying vital cover for the breeding geese. Yet the nene survived, and there were at least 25,000 of them at the end of the 18th century, when Europeans reached the islands. The new settlers introduced more killers: black rats, cats, and in 1883 the small Indian mongoose. They also had guns; between them human hunters and predators eliminated the nene from the lowlands.

Kauai
Oahu
Hawaii
(UNITED STATES)
Maui
Hawaii

DATA PANEL

Nene (Hawaiian goose)

Branta sandvicensis

Family: Anatidae

World population: About 960–1,000

Distribution: Originally throughout Hawaiian archipelago, but reduced to a few wild birds on Hawaii by 1950; following reintroductions, it now lives wild on Hawaii, Maui, and Kauai

Habitat: Grassy shrublands and sparsely vegetated, semiarid basalt lava flows on volcanic slopes; lowland pasture on Kauai

Size: Length: 25–27 in (63–69 cm). Weight: 2.9–6.6 lb (1.3–3 kg)

Form: Small, erect goose with short wings, long legs, and strong feet with reduced webbing. Black bill, face, and crown; golden-buff neck with unique dark furrows; upperparts and breast sepia brown with pattern of dark gray and white; white belly

Diet: Moist vegetation such as grass, leaves and berries, and seeds

Breeding: Birds pair for life and breed in November–January; 3–5 white eggs laid in a nest scrape and incubated by female for about 4 weeks while male stands guard; young fledge in about 10–12 weeks

Related endangered species: In Hawaiian Islands, Laysan duck (*Anas laysanensis*) VU; Hawaiian duck (*A. wyvilliana*) EN. Other threatened geese include the lesser white-fronted goose (*Anser erythropus*) VU and the red-breasted goose (*Branta ruficollis*) VU

Status: IUCN VU; CITES I

See also: Introductions **1:** 54; Captive Breeding **1:** 87; Reintroduction **1:** 92; Duck, Labrador **4:** 42; Swan, Trumpeter **9:** 44

By 1907, when hunting was banned, the nene was probably found only on Hawaii itself. It had retreated into the volcanic uplands where mongoose and cats were scarce, yet while the near-barren slopes provided enough food for bare survival, the extra nutrients needed for producing eggs and feeding young were often lacking. In poor seasons many adult geese failed to breed, and the young birds that did hatch often died from malnutrition. By 1949 there were perhaps only 30 left.

Rescue

The recovery of the nene is almost entirely due to captive breeding. In 1950 three birds were acquired by what is now the Wildfowl and Wetlands Trust at Slimbridge, England, and they became the foundation of a captive-bred flock of 2,000 or so. Meanwhile, the birds were also being bred in captivity on Hawaii. In 1960 a reintroduction program started, and since then over 2,300 geese have been released into protected areas on Hawaii and the neighboring island of Maui.

On Hawaii and Maui the reintroduced nene live in the uplands, where they still suffer from bad weather and malnutrition. On Hawaii the nene population of about 400 has to be boosted by new introductions and given extra food. On Maui the population of about 280 is stable or growing.

Since 1985 some 137 nene have been introduced to the more distant island of Kauai. There the population has more than doubled to over 260. There is no mongoose predation, allowing the nene to live in the coastal lowlands, where they enjoy a better diet.

Conservation bodies aim to establish large, predator-free reserves in lowland areas. The elimination of poaching and reduction of roadkills are also planned. If coupled with translocations of stock between islands to minimize inbreeding, the nene may be on track for a full recovery.

The nene is a relative of the Canada goose. It evolved on the Hawaiian Islands into a species with shortened wings and half-webbed feet.

Newt, Great Crested

Triturus cristatus

Although the great crested newt is widely distributed across Europe, the species has declined over much of its range. Changes in land use and agricultural practices over the last 50 years have destroyed much of its pond and woodland habitat.

The great crested newt of northwestern Europe—along with other European newts of the genus *Triturus*—gets its name from the large, deeply notched crest that runs along the back of the breeding male. The European newts are unique among tailed amphibians: During the breeding season the males develop elaborate decorations that serve to attract and stimulate females during courtship.

Although great crested newts spend much of their lives on land, breeding takes place in water. Adults migrate to ponds in early spring. Females start the breeding season already full of large, yolk-filled eggs. It takes the males several weeks to fully develop their deep tail and crest, features that play an important part in the mating process. Males that emerge from their winter hibernation with larger fat reserves develop larger crests, and it is likely that they are more attractive to females.

Mating usually occurs at dusk. The male takes up a position in front of the female and displays to her with rhythmic beats of his tail. If the female responds by moving toward him, the male deposits a package of sperm, called a spermatophore, on the floor of the pond. The female then moves over it and picks it up with her open cloaca (cavity into which the genital ducts open).

Two or three days after mating the female begins to lay her eggs, a process that takes many weeks. Great crested newts usually produce between 150 and 200 eggs, each of which is laid individually and carefully wrapped in the leaf of a water plant. After two to three weeks the eggs hatch into tiny larvae, which, once they have used up their reserves of yolk, start to feed on tiny aquatic animals, such as water fleas. Larval development takes two to three months, and the young emerge from their pond as miniature adults in late summer and fall. Females mate several times during the breeding season, interrupting egg-laying to replenish their supplies of sperm.

Risk Factors

Together with its close relative, the marbled newt, the great crested newt has a remarkable abnormality of its chromosomes. As a result, 50 percent of its young die as early embryos. This is one reason, perhaps, why crested newts have declined more rapidly than other European newt species.

Predation is not a significant problem for great crested newts. When handled, glands in their skin produce a bitter, milky secretion that humans and potential predators, such as water birds and hedgehogs, find highly distasteful. In addition, the bright orange and black pattern on the belly appears to warn off predators.

However, crested newts are at risk from habitat alteration and destruction. The main problem has been changes in land use since World War II. Woodlands have been cleared, hedges destroyed, and land drained to make way for

See also: Drainage and Irrigation **1:** 40; Pesticides **1:** 51; Olm **7:** 24

crops and livestock. Ponds, which were a common feature of the European landscape, have been filled in. In some parts of Britain, for example, 90 percent of farm ponds have disappeared in the last 50 years.

Another threat to crested and other newt species comes from fish that eat newt larvae. The eggs and larvae of crested newts are also sensitive to a variety of pollutants, such as herbicides and pesticides.

In the southern parts of its range the crested newt is found in a number of forms that differ from the northern form in having longer bodies, shorter legs, and a different shape of crest on the male. Such forms are now recognized as three distinct species: the Italian crested newt, the Danube newt, and the southern crested newt. All are threatened by habitat loss and protected, to varying degrees, by national and European laws.

At the southwestern edge of its distribution, however, the crested newt is expanding its range. In some parts of France it appears to be adapting to new patterns of land use and is even spreading into ponds previously used only by marbled newts.

DATA PANEL

Great crested newt (warty newt)

Triturus cristatus

Family: Salamandridae

World population: Unknown

Distribution: Northwestern Europe

Habitat: Woodland, scrub, and hedgerows close to ponds, lakes, or ditches

Size: Length: male 3.9–5.5 in (10–14 cm); female 3.9–6.3 in (10–16 cm)

Form: Dark gray or brown newt with large black spots on upperside; bright orange underside with black spots. In breeding season male (only) has large, dorsal crest and deep tail with white stripe

Diet: Small invertebrates

Breeding: Mates in spring and early summer. Between 70 and 600 (usually 150–200) eggs laid; larvae hatch after 2-week gestation; young develop over 2–3 months. Life span up to 16 years

Related endangered species: Danube newt *(Triturus dobrogicus)* DD

Status: IUCN LRcd; not listed by CITES

In the breeding season *the male great crested newt develops a distinctive crest and tail, which he displays during courtship. The tail has a conspicuous white stripe that shows up clearly in the dim light of dusk—when mating occurs.*

Numbat

Myrmecobius fasciatus

From an all-time low of fewer than 1,000 animals in the 1970s, the numbat has begun a slow recovery. However, changes in land use and the presence of many nonnative predators in Australia mean that the species will almost certainly never be as widespread as it once was.

The numbat is an unusual marsupial in many ways. It is the only living member of the group that is not even partly nocturnal, and the only one that feeds exclusively on insects. In fact, the numbat's daytime activity and its diet are interlinked. Despite its alternative names of banded or marsupial anteater, it feeds chiefly on termites, which it collects from the many tunnels and galleries that the insects create in pieces of dead wood. The termites are active during the daytime, and the numbat tailors its activity to its prey. A single numbat can consume an incredible 20,000 termites a day.

The numbat is also rather unusual looking compared with other animals. It is much more strikingly marked than most other marsupials, with six or seven bright white bars across its rump and a dark stripe on each side of its face. With such striking features it is hardly surprising that the numbat has won a special place in people's affections. It is now the official state animal of Western Australia.

Imported Predators

The biggest problem for the numbat, as for many other native Australian animals, has been the introduction of new predators—such as cats, dogs, and foxes—by European settlers. Research has shown that foxes have been almost entirely responsible for the numbat's decline. Two or three hundred years ago the animal was widespread throughout much of southern Australia; its range probably covered about a quarter of the continent. By the mid-1920s numbats appeared to have completely died out in South Australia, and by 1960 there were just two remnant populations in Western Australia, close to Perth.

Quite how the two populations managed to survive in Western Australia, having died out everywhere else, is an interesting question with a simple but logical answer. The numbat used to live in almost any region where it could find termites. When the continent of Australia was invaded by introduced predators, the numbat could survive

DATA PANEL

Numbat (banded anteater, marsupial anteater, walpurti)

Myrmecobius fasciatus

Family: Myrmecobiidae

World population: Several thousand

Distribution: Southwestern Australia

Habitat: Dry, open woodlands such as eucalyptus forests

Size: Length head/body: 7–11 in (17.5–27.5 cm); tail: 5.5–6.5 in (13–17 cm). Weight: 10–20 oz (280–550 g)

Form: Distinctive-looking mammal with long, furry tail and strong, clawed feet; grayish body fur tinged red on upper back, fading to creamy gray beneath; back and rump marked with 6 or 7 striking white bars; long,

pointed muzzle, small black nose; ears erect; eyes large and black; dark stripe across sides of face and through eyes

Diet: Mostly ants and termites, plus some other insects

Breeding: Between 2 and 4 young born December–April; young spend 4 months hidden in long fur of mother's belly, attached to her teats. Independent at about 9 months. May live as long as 6 years

Related endangered species: No close relatives

Status: IUCN VU; not listed by CITES

AUSTRALIA

Western Australia

See also: Introductions **1:** 54; Natural Disasters **1:** 57

only in areas where there were both termites and secure hiding places. The best refuges for numbats are hollow logs. However, while many trees rot and fall apart, making good termite hunting grounds, only some hollow out when they die. One is the wandoo tree found in Western Australia. Fortunately for the numbat, wandoos provide plentiful hollow trunks, logs, and branches, offering both shelter and a healthy supply of termites.

Habitat Problems and Solutions

Another problem for numbats was an increase in the number of forest fires. Native people used to carefully burn small patches of vegetation each year as a means of reducing the volume of dry, inflammable material. However, when they left the land, the practice ceased. Old dead plant material accumulated; and if it caught light naturally by being struck by lightning, the resulting fires were fierce and hot. Many animals died, and the termites and their rotting logs disappeared along with them.

The numbat *is the only survivor of an entire marsupial family. Its striking coat pattern and daytime activity make it one of the more conspicuous Australian mammals.*

Clearance of land for agriculture also destroyed much good numbat habitat. In some areas trees were felled for timber or fuel, leaving no deadwood at all. The campaign to save the animal has therefore taken two main approaches. One goal has been to create and preserve numbat-friendly woodland, with plenty of dead wood suitable for termites; the other has been the eradication from these areas of nonnative predators, especially foxes.

Under such conditions the numbats are thriving. They have even been reintroduced successfully into a reserve where the species had become extinct in the 1970s. Reintroduction into other areas is now an important priority; increasing the number of stable populations will reduce the risk that a local disaster, such as an epidemic disease or wildfire, could wipe out the entire species at a single blow.

Nuthatch, Algerian

Sitta ledanti

Known to science only since 1975, the tree-dwelling Algerian nuthatch is Algeria's only endemic bird species. It exists in small, declining populations that are restricted to one small area; its future depends on reversing habitat destruction and preventing further disturbance.

It is hardly surprising that the discovery of the Algerian nuthatch in 1975 should have amazed ornithologists, since it was the first new bird species to be found in the Palearctic zoogeographical region (including Europe, North and Central Asia, and North Africa) since 1937. What is puzzling is the fact that the bird had remained unknown for so long, although its limited distribution in the little-known mountain forests helped account for its elusiveness.

The bird was found by the Belgian botanist Jean-Pierre Ledant and two companions when they climbed the 6,545-foot (1,995-m) Djebel Babor, a peak in the Petite Kabylie Mountains in northern Algeria. The group had set out to study the Algerian fir, an endemic tree species that still grew in an isolated remnant of forest on the upper slopes of the mountain. The discovery came as they neared the top and saw a bird that they recognized as a nuthatch. At the time the only records of nuthatches ever having occurred in Algeria were some 19th-century reports of Eurasian nuthatches spotted 185 miles (300 km) to the west of the newly discovered bird. In fact, the Djebel Babor specimen more closely resembled a species of nuthatch endemic to Corsica.

Mystery Bird

At first Ledant was unsure of the true significance of his find, but he communicated it to the French ornithologist Jacques Vielliard, a nuthatch specialist. Skeptical at first, Vielliard encouraged Ledant to return to Algeria to search for the mystery bird. Ledant made two unsuccessful visits, but on a third trip in 1976—in company with Vielliard—the two men watched the new species for several days and collected a breeding male and female. In 1975 there were estimated to be just 12 nuthatch pairs in Djebel Babor, but by 1982 the estimate was revised to about 80 pairs.

Fifteen years after Ledant's original visit other investigators found a second population of Algerian nuthatches in deciduous and evergreen oak forest in Taza National Park, situated on the Guerrouch Massif 12 miles (20 km) from the Babor Forest and at a much lower altitude. Provisional estimates put this newly

DATA PANEL

Algerian nuthatch

Sitta ledanti

Family: Sittidae

World population: 1,000–2,500 birds

Distribution: Northeastern Algeria

Habitat: Oak forest on mountain summits at about 6,500 ft (2,000 m); regenerating oak forest from 2,900–4,600 ft (900–1,400 m)

Size: Length: 5 in (13 cm). Weight: 0.6 oz (16–18 g)

Form: Small, dumpy bird with a relatively large head. Slender, mainly black bill with wedge-shaped tip; short tail. Upperparts blue-gray with bold whitish stripe above each eye; blackish stripe on cap, forecrown, and through eye in males and to a lesser extent in females; underparts creamy-pink to orange-buff; gray legs and feet

Diet: In summer mainly insects and spiders with some seeds; in winter mainly seeds and nuts of trees

Breeding: May to June. Nest of woodchips, leaves, feathers, and hog bristles prepared in a tree hole 10–50 ft (3–15 m) above ground, usually in dead fir or cedar, but also in oaks. Most common brood size is 2, with a maximum of 4; incubation period not recorded; fledging time probably 3–3.5 weeks

Related endangered species: White-browed nuthatch (*Sitta victoriae*) EN; giant nuthatch (*S. magna*) VU; beautiful nuthatch (*S. formosa*) VU

Status: IUCN EN; not listed by CITES

discovered population at about 350 individuals. The find showed that the species was not restricted to remnant cedar and cedar-and-fir forests like the one on the Djebel Babor, as had been assumed. The discovery prompted further searches in oak forests in the Taza region.

In 1990 two more colonies were discovered at Tamentout and Djimla, both within 6 miles (10 km) of the two previously known sites. These populations currently remain uncounted, but they are unlikely to exceed those at Taza. Although the estimates may be overcautious, it is still possible that there are fewer than 1,000 Algerian nuthatches in the world.

Trouble on the Slopes

Although the Djebel Babor lies within a national park, the nuthatch population there is not entirely secure. Fires have reduced the area of original native forest on the mountain slopes. As a result, the rich mix of species that once populated it has disappeared, giving way to a poorer habitat dominated by cedars.

To add to the problems confronting the birds, large numbers of livestock graze the hillsides, preventing the trees from regenerating and impoverishing the understory of shrubs and saplings. At the same time, woodcutting removes some of the birds' potential nest sites. To make matters worse, a track was laid up the mountain in the 1970s to provide vehicle access to the upper slopes. The resulting traffic has already caused erosion in the area. Disturbance from tourists and an increase in the risk of forest fires can also be added to the list of threats.

On the bright side, the nuthatch is listed as a protected species in Algeria, and the largest surviving population—in the Taza National Park—is effectively

The Algerian nuthatch, *like other nuthatches, is an agile climber; unlike other tree-dwelling birds, it can move down as well as up tree trunks.*

managed and not considered to be at risk from habitat loss. To build on this record of success, conservationists are now targeting the Djebel Babor population, believed to be in decline. Their goals include finding new ways of conserving the dwindling forest remnants with the help of local people, carrying out a program of reforestation on the mountain's southern slopes, establishing plantations outside the forest in order to reduce the pressure for firewood, and controlling tourism in the surrounding area.

17

Nyala, Mountain

Tragelaphus buxtoni

Unknown until the early 20th century, the mountain nyala is a species of African antelope found only in the Bale Mountains of southeastern Ethiopia. There may now be only 2,000 left.

Ethiopia was an area of Africa not exploited by the West during the 19th century, since the terrain is mountainous and offered little scope for colonial expansion. Consequently, many species evaded discovery, especially in the higher mountains, where there were no roads and few people. The mountain nyala was one of the last large mammals to be discovered in Africa and was unknown to scientists until 1908.

Nyalas are antelopes found in southeast African forests. The mountain nyala, a similar and related animal, used to be found all over the higher ground of southeastern Ethiopia, but is now confined to the Bale Mountains in the south, in areas above 10,000 feet (3,000 m). It generally lives in small, loosely organized groups and feeds by browsing on the trees and shrubs that grow in the mountains up to the edge of the alpine moors at about 13,000 feet (4,200 m).

Mountain nyalas are fond of giant St. John's wort, which forms dense thickets, but they also nibble at small herbs such as lady's mantle and goose grass. The nyalas are normally active at dawn and dusk, spending the rest of the day under the cover of trees. They do not wander very far and may spend most of their time within a few adjacent valleys, occupying an area of less than about 4 square miles (10 sq. km). Occasionally, adult males, which are sometimes solitary, will wander more widely.

Hostile Homeland

Mountain nyalas are well adapted to contend with a harsh environment in which temperatures fall well below freezing every

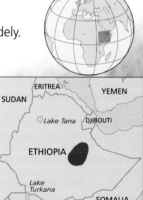

DATA PANEL	
Mountain nyala *Tragelaphus buxtoni* **Family:** Bovidae **World population:** Fewer than 3,000 **Distribution:** Ethiopia: Bale Mountains **Habitat:** Mountain heaths and forests **Size:** Length: male 7.5 ft (2.4–2.6 m); female 6 ft (1.9–2.0 m); height at shoulder: 36–54 in (91–137 cm). Weight: 330–650 lb (150–300 kg) **Form:** Large, slender antelope with a hairy crest along the back and down the throat. The male has spiral horns, sometimes over 36 in (90 cm) long. Males are dark brown, becoming darker with age, with prominent white marks on their face and flanks; females are paler	**Diet:** Various plants, mostly shrubs, but sometimes grass and lichens; dead leaves in the dry season **Breeding:** Mating mainly in December; a single calf is born after 8–9 months at the end of the wet season. Life span unknown, but likely to exceed 10 years **Related endangered species:** Greater kudu *(Tragelaphus strepsiceros)** LRcd **Status:** IUCN EN; not listed by CITES

See also: Pasture **1:** 38; Kudu, Greater **6:** 16; Wolf, Ethiopian **10:** 64

night. However, the moorlands can be too exposed even for them, and during the dry season they have to migrate to areas at lower altitudes where temperatures are higher and food more abundant.

In recent years the mountain nyalas have suffered from the conversion of land for grazing domestic sheep, goats, and cattle, which remove all the suitable fodder. The expanding human population has also encroached on much of the nyala's forest. Trees have been chopped down for firewood, and many areas are now burned regularly to encourage grass to grow for domestic stock to eat. Since grass alone is not an adequate food for the nyala, it has been forced to retreat from large areas of its range, and it now occupies only those higher areas of the mountains that are unsuitable for farming.

In the past the nyala has also suffered from hunting by local people and occasional big-game hunters. However, the species is now legally protected, so the latter is no longer a problem.

In the 1960s there were thought to be as many as 8,000 mountain nyala, but the latest estimate (1996) suggests that there may be as few as 2,000 left. At least half the remaining mountain nyala population is confined to the Bale Mountains National Park, where they are relatively safe. There are no mountain nyalas in captivity.

The mountain nyala *is larger than the nyalas of southeastern Africa. It is grayish-brown, with white markings on its head, neck, and body.*

Ocelot, Texas

Leopardus pardalis albescens

Ocelots face problems like those of other predators with highly valued skins. The Texas subspecies is at the very edge of the ocelot's overall range and so is particularly vulnerable.

Like many other cats, the ocelot is nocturnal and will travel several miles a night in search of food. The adult males are solitary and have large territories that overlap the home ranges of several females. Youngsters live with their mother for a year after birth; the males then disperse, sometimes displacing their father, while young females more often stay close to where they were born. They are capable of breeding at about two years of age, but they rarely produce more than two kittens per year.

The ocelot enjoys a wide distribution throughout much of Central and South America. Like many other species with an extensive range through many very different types of habitat, the ocelot has formed distinct subspecies at the edges of its distribution, in Texas. The closely related jaguarundi also has a Texan subspecies—*Herpailurus yagaurondi cacomitli*. The jaguarundis reach the edge of their range in Texas,

and here a local subspecies has formed. The Texan jaguarundi, like the Texan ocelot, is listed by the IUCN as Endangered.

Living at the Edge

Animals living at the edge of their main range are at the limits of what they can tolerate. They are especially vulnerable to habitat changes or population disturbance, such as a high death toll as a result of hunting pressures.

Throughout its range the ocelot has been hunted for its beautiful fur. During the 1960s and 1970s hundreds of thousands of ocelots were killed for their skins. Coats made from ocelot pelts used to sell for tens of thousands of dollars, although trade has been curtailed as a result of the CITES restrictions imposed in 1989.

In addition, much of the ocelot's natural habitat in the United States was lost as farmland was extended, and cattle ranching created grassland out of bush. Ocelots were also mistakenly regarded as a threat to farm animals, although they are actually too small to be much of a danger to anything larger than a chicken. However, despite being relatively harmless, ocelots were still shot or trapped. Ocelots became rare everywhere as a result of excessive exploitation. In the southern United States additional losses caused by hunting and habitat loss could not easily be sustained by an animal living precariously on the extreme edge of its natural range. The combination of such pressures, coupled with the ocelot's inability to

---

DATA PANEL

Texas ocelot

Leopardus pardalis albescens

Family: Felidae

World population: Unknown; perhaps only a few hundred

Distribution: Central and South America, but Texas subspecies only in southwestern Texas and adjacent parts of Mexico

Habitat: Rocky areas with dense thorn scrub

Size: Length head/body: 27–35 in (65–85 cm); tail: 13–15 in (31–36 cm); male usually a little bigger than female. Weight: 20–40 lb (9–18 kg)

Form: Small, grayish cat with dark, dappled markings and a long tail

Diet: Small mammals and birds; also fish, insects, even land crabs

Breeding: Two kittens, born in fall. Life span at least 13 years

Related endangered species: Iberian lynx *(Lynx pardinus)** EN; various other cats

Status IUCN EN; CITES I

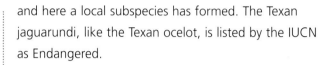

UNITED STATES
Texas
Louisiana
MEXICO

See also: Luxury Products **1:** 46; Jaguar **5:** 86; Leopard, Snow **6:** 32; Panther, Florida **7:** 54

Ocelots *have distinctive dark, dappled markings. Kittens were sometimes captured and kept as pets, and ocelots are still a popular attraction in zoos.*

breed any faster, started the decline into extinction. It has now disappeared from Arkansas, Louisiana, Arizona, and eastern Texas, leaving only two small populations in southeastern Texas. Occasionally individuals also stray over the border from Mexico.

If the dangers or threats are removed, local losses can often be made good by natural spread from the main population or by reintroductions. However, the disappearance of a local subspecies is a loss. Any spread or reintroductions involve other subspecies. They may be similar, but they are not the same, and the species as a whole will be genetically poorer.

The ocelot's preservation is also a matter of national pride. The United States is a prosperous country and should not allow any of its animals to die out or become vulnerable without making some

attempt to protect them. Texas is now the last home for the ocelot in the country. Efforts have been made to protect the animal from persecution and from trade within the United States. A recovery plan for the wild cats of Texas and Arizona is in place, the main aim of which is to sustain the population of ocelots in Texas. The plan includes provision for raising the profile of the animal through publicity and promotion of research into its biology and conservation.

Scientific estimates suggest that ocelot populations need to have at least 1,300 animals in order to avoid inbreeding. It is unlikely that the small areas of Texas where they still occur are home to that many, so the future for the subspecies is uncertain. However, it seems that the rest of the species is secure in protected areas of its range across South America.

Okapi

Okapia johnstoni

The okapi was not discovered until the early 20th century, before which its dense forest habitat was largely unexplored. Today, as a result of civil war and the consequent migration of people into remote areas, the future of the okapi hangs in the balance.

Although the okapi was known to the pygmy people of the Ituri Forest in Zaire (now the Democratic Republic of Congo) for generations, its forest home was so dense and unexplored that nobody in the outside world knew of the animal's existence. It was the American explorer H. M. Stanley (1841–1904) who brought the animal to public attention, having been told about it by the local people. The first specimens were officially described in 1901, but it was not until 1918 that live animals arrived in Europe. Originally mistaken for some kind of forest zebra, the okapi is in fact a type of giraffe.

The okapi lives in the forests of the upper Zaire River basin, up to about 3,300 feet (1,000 m) above sea level. It lives alone or in small family groups. Its home range covers an area of about 2 square miles (5 sq. km). Each day it walks short distances in search of food, following regularly used trails. Males may travel farther, especially when seeking a mate.

Okapis eat over 100 different types of forest plant, salt-laden soils, and even charcoal from burned tree stumps. They mark their trails with scent but do not appear to occupy exclusive territories. Young are born between August and October, at the end of the wet season. The okapi has little to fear from natural predators, except perhaps the leopard.

In the past the okapi was hunted or trapped by local people for its meat. This relatively low level of harvesting is unlikely to have posed a significant threat to the total population. Big-game hunting was even less of a threat because the okapi's forest home was so remote and difficult to penetrate. In addition, the Belgian colonial government gave okapis legal protection in 1933.

Land Clearance

In more recent times human activity has put the okapi at risk. People needing pasture for cattle and sheep have made clearings in the forest by burning the forest vegetation. While bush fires prevented new

DATA PANEL

Okapi

Okapia johnstoni

Family: Giraffidae

World population: Unknown, but likely to be only a few thousand at most

Distribution: Upper part of Zaire River basin in the Democratic Republic of Congo (formerly Zaire)

Habitat: Dense forests and jungles

Size: Length: 6.5–7 ft (1.9–2.1 m); height at shoulder: 5–5.5 ft (1.5–1.8 m); males a little smaller than females. Weight: 460–550 lb (210–250 kg)

Form: Chocolate-brown animal with white "socks" and stripes on legs and rump. Two small furry "horns" on its forehead. Shoulders higher than hips; thick neck. Long, blue-gray tongue

Diet: Shrubs, fruit, ferns, and fungi

Breeding: One young born each year; stays with its mother for 6 months; mature at about 3 years. Life span 15–20 years in the wild; over 30 years in captivity

Related endangered species: Reticulated giraffe (*Giraffa camelopardalis reticulata*)* LRcd

Status: IUCN LRnt; not listed by CITES

See also: Pasture 1: 38; War 1: 47; Giraffe, Reticulated 5: 30; Kudu, Greater 6: 16

forest growth, the grass attracted greater numbers of antelope, which displaced the okapis. As a result of land clearance, the okapi's distribution is less widespread than it used to be. It no longer includes western Uganda, for example, having contracted to just one part of the Congo Basin.

Unstable Environment

Although the numbers of okapis may be fairly high in places, with one animal per 0.8 to 1.2 square miles (2 to 3 sq. km), the total area over which the species lives is limited, so the population as a whole is vulnerable when things go wrong. In 1992 the Okapi Wildlife Reserve, which covers 5,289 square miles (13,700 sq. km), was created with a view to providing greater protection for the native wildlife. However, the reserve was unpopular with local people, who thought that it restricted their traditional activities. In recent years there has also been a huge increase in the market for bush meat, and this is a further threat to the okapi.

In the 1990s political instability led to civil war in Zaire. An increasing number of okapis were shot for food by hungry people fleeing from threats of massacre. In addition, migrations of refugees sought sanctuary in forest areas that had previously been undisturbed by humans. The effect on the okapis (and other wildlife of the region) is not yet known, but is likely to have been detrimental.

The okapi, *like its close relative the giraffe, has small protruberances, or "horns," covered by furry skin on its head. The animal was originally mistaken for some kind of forest zebra because of its partly striped coat.*

Olm

Proteus anguinus

A bizarre, permanently aquatic salamander that lives almost entirely underground, the olm is vulnerable to a variety of factors that threaten its restricted and specialized habitat.

The olm is a strange and obscure amphibian. It is highly adapted to a habitat of underground streams, pools, and lakes, and shows a classic example of pedomorphism. This is an evolutionary change that results in the retention of juvenile characteristics in the adult form. The species does not exist as a terrestrial, lung-breathing salamander. During the course of its normal pattern of development the olm has become "frozen" in the larval stage, retaining the large, feathery external gills and laterally compressed tail, which it beats to propel itself through the water.

Adapted for Life in the Dark

The olm's underground streams and pools occur in the "karst" landscape that is associated with limestone.

Living in permanent darkness, it has only tiny rudimentary eyes that are covered by skin. Its larvae, on the other hand, have quite well-developed eyes, but they degenerate during life. The adults lack dark pigment in their skin, but vary in color, being white, pink, gray, or yellowy; younger individuals often have darker blotches on the skin.

Unable to see, the olm must rely on other senses to find its food and for social communication. It has an excellent sense of smell, and its skin contains large numbers of tiny lateral line organs that are sensitive to water-borne vibrations. It uses its sense of smell and sensitivity to vibrations to detect the moving invertebrates on which it feeds. These senses are also important during aggressive interactions between males and during courtship and mating.

As recently as 1994 a distinct form of the olm has been discovered. Given the status of a subspecies, *Proteus anguinus parkelj* is black, has well-developed eyes, and is found only in the Bela Krajuna region of southeastern Slovenia. Individuals have been observed emerging from caves at night and swimming around in open pools and streams.

Breeding

Living underground, the olm is not exposed to the seasonal variations in temperature and rainfall that are experienced by amphibians living on the surface. Water temperature in its cave habitat is more or less constant all year round. As a result, the olm has no obvious breeding season but may breed at any time of year. When breeding, the slightly smaller

DATA PANEL

Olm (blind cave salamander)

Proteus anguinus

Family: Proteidae

World population: Unknown

Distribution: Southeastern Europe: the Adriatic coast from northern Italy to Montenegro (former Yugoslavia)

Habitat: Caves and underground lakes and streams in limestone mountains

Size: Length: 8–11 in (20–28 cm)

Form: Large, flat head with rounded snout; white, pale-gray, pink, or creamy-yellow elongated body; darker blotches in younger animals; large pink, feathery external gills. Small rudimentary limbs

Diet: Small aquatic invertebrates, mainly crustaceans

Breeding: Any time of year. Eggs fertilized internally. Twelve to 70 eggs laid under a stone and guarded by female until hatched; alternatively, just 1–2 eggs develop inside body of female, who gives birth to well-developed larvae. Young mature at 7 years. Life span up to 58 years

Related endangered species: None

Status: IUCN VU; not listed by CITES

males become aggressive toward one another, defending their territory. If a female enters a male's territory, he performs a tail-fanning display—similar to that of European newts—in which he beats the tip of his tail rapidly against his flank. This creates a water current that he directs toward the female, who receives both vibratory stimuli and odor cues. If she is sexually responsive, she will approach the male. He then turns away, stopping to deposit a packet of sperm (called a spermatophore) on the ground. The female follows him and passes over the spermatophore. As she does so, her cloaca (cavity in the pelvic region into which the genital ducts open) passes over the spermatophore, and the sperm is drawn up into her body.

The female then creates a simple nest in the debris on the cave floor and lays a clutch of eggs. She guards them against predators until they hatch. Alternatively, between one and two eggs develop inside the body of the female, who gives birth to well-developed larvae.

The olm lacks any dark pigment. Instead, individuals show a variety of pale colors, from pink to creamy yellow.

Habitat at Risk

The olm's specialized habitat requirements—places where there are underground caves containing water—mean that even under ideal conditions it will always be a rare species.

Although it is reasonably safe from many of the changes that have adversely affected surface-living amphibians, such as habitat destruction, it is not wholly unaffected by events on the surface. Much of the water that fills the underground caves flows in from the surface, where it can become contaminated by a range of pollutants, such as agricultural runoff or industrial waste. It is believed that pollution is a major factor in the reduction of the olm population.

The olm is a fascinating animal, both to scientists and to amateur enthusiasts. In the past olms were collected as pig food. Today it is collection by enthusiasts that is having a more serious effect on natural populations.

Orang-Utan

Pongo pygmaeus

Orang-utan means "man of the forest" in the Malay language. Once numbering hundreds of thousands, the orang-utan population has declined sharply in recent years because of loss of habitat and capture for the pet trade.

The orang-utan holds two animal records: It is the world's largest tree-dwelling mammal, and it is the only great ape that lives in Asia. Living in the trees of the tropical rain forests of Borneo and Sumatra, this ape rarely walks on the ground. It has very long, strong arms ideally suited to a life of swinging and climbing from branch to branch in the tree canopy.

Orang-utans tend to live alone or in very small groups. Most nights they build a fresh nest in the trees, only occasionally reusing a nest. Two-thirds of their diet is fruit—especially wild figs and durians —but they have a huge appetite and may spend a whole day sitting gorging in a tree.

Orang-utans can live for up to 40 years; they are mature aged between seven and 10. Females normally give birth to a single baby, though occasionally they have twins. The babies are completely dependent on the mother and are not weaned until three years old.

Decline and Fall

Once orang-utans were found throughout Southeast Asia and southern China, but today there are estimated to be fewer than 30,000 in the wild. Their numbers have declined by 30 to 50 percent in the last 10 years.

The greatest threat to orang-utans is the destruction of their habitat—tropical rain forest. Large areas of forest have been affected as trees are felled for their timber, and land cleared for farming. It is estimated that 80 percent of all forest in Malaysia and Indonesia has already been logged. In the 1990s a series of forest fires that burned for months at a time badly affected the orang-utan.

Another threat is the capture of live orangs for the pet trade. Despite legislation, it is estimated that between 1996 and 2000 about 1,000 orang-utans were captured to be sold as exotic pets. For every orang-utan that survives capture and shipment, five or six others will die in the process.

The highly intelligent species is protected by law in Indonesia and Malaysia; both countries have signed up

---

DATA PANEL

Orang-utan

Pongo pygmaeus

Family: Pongidae

World population: Fewer than 30,000

Distribution: Indonesia (Kalimantan, Sumatra) and Malaysia (Sabah, Sarawak)

Habitat: Tropical rain forests

Size: Height: male 54 in (137 cm); female 45 in (115 cm). Weight: male 130–200 lb (60–90 kg); female 88–110 lb (40–50 kg)

Form: A large long-haired ape; the coat is usually a reddish color but varies from orange to dark chocolate

Diet: Mainly fruit; also young leaves and shoots, insects, bark, and small mammals

Breeding: Usually gives birth to single young; mature at 7–10 years. Life span up to 40 years

Related endangered species: Lowland gorilla (*Gorilla gorilla gorilla*)* EN; mountain gorilla (*G. g. beringei*)* EN; pygmy chimpanzee (*Pan paniscus*)* EN; chimpanzee (*P. troglodytes*)* EN

Status: IUCN EN; CITES I

See also: Exploitation of Live Animals **1:** 49; Chimpanzee **3:** 42; Gorilla, Western Lowland **5:** 40; Monkey, Proboscis **6:** 90

to CITES. The 1987 Asian Primate Action Plan identified several conservation measures needed to protect the orang-utan. They included the setting up and managing of protected areas (such as the Gunung National Park in Sumatra), surveys to establish the population and distribution of orang-utans, and a public education program. About 60 percent of orang-utans in Borneo could be protected if conservation laws were more rigorously enforced.

There are a number of orang-utan rehabilitation centers. They look after orang-utans rescued from smugglers or those that have lost their homes because of logging. The apes are relocated to protected areas. There are about 645 orang-utans (1992 figures) held in 142 zoos and collections worldwide—of which 492 were born in captivity.

Orang-utans *are fascinating apes that share 96.4 percent of the genes that make up the human genetic code.*

Oryx, Arabian

Oryx leucoryx

In the vast deserts of the Middle East the oryx was hunted to extinction in the 1970s. It has now been reintroduced to the wild from captive herds bred in zoos.

Arabian oryx live in small herds, usually with fewer than 10 animals per group, which lessens the impact of their feeding on the sparse desert vegetation. They generally feed early in the day, then rest, and feed again before finding shade for the hottest part of the afternoon. The animals move around seasonally between feeding places and may use a total area of several thousand square miles in a year. They seem able to detect rain at a distance; they travel to the area affected to feed on the new growth of plants. Oryx prefer rocky or stony plains to soft sand and steep mountains.

Big-game hunters used to pursue oryx for trophies, and for generations the animals were hunted

DATA PANEL

Arabian oryx (white oryx)

Oryx leucoryx

Family: Bovidae

World population: Over 2,000, most in captivity

Distribution: Formerly in Egypt, Iraq, Israel, Syria, United Arab Emirates, and Yemen. Reintroduced to Jordan, Oman, and Saudi Arabia

Habitat: Rocky and stony plains in desert areas

Size: Length: 5–5.5 ft (1.5–1.6 m); height at shoulder: 32–41 in (81–104 cm). Weight: 140–155 lb (65–70 kg)

Form: A white antelope with black legs, each with a white band above

the hoof. Horns (in both sexes) are straight, about 24 in (60 cm) long

Diet: Grasses and desert shrubs, from which they also get most of the water they need (although they may sometimes travel to a water hole)

Breeding: Births can occur in any month after 8-month gestation. The single calf stays with its mother for 4–5 months. Females are mature at about 3 years. Life span can be over 20 years

Related endangered species: Scimitar-horned oryx *(Oryx dammah)** EW

Status: IUCN EN; CITES I

by men riding on camels. Although some escaped, many did not, and they were steadily eliminated from countries such as Syria, Egypt, and Israel. By the 1950s the increased availability of four-wheel drive vehicles, abundant fuel, automatic rifles, and oil-based local wealth combined to make hunting in Arab countries both more widespread and more efficient. Gunmen in vehicles hunted the animals to extinction. The last wild oryx were killed in the 1970s.

Rescue Remedy

Fortunately, several Arab countries had already made efforts to keep and breed the oryx in captivity. In 1962 international cooperation between zoos made it possible to assemble a

See also: Reintroduction 1: 92; Oryx, Scimitar-Horned 7:

few animals in Phoenix, Arizona (where the climate is very similar to that of the native home of the Arabian oryx), from which to breed animals specifically for release back into the wild. This was the first such international project for any endangered or extinct species, and it has been highly successful. Oryx were released in Oman in 1982, Jordan in 1983, and Saudi Arabia in 1990. There are now over 500 oryx living wild in those three areas, and many more in zoos (such as that in Los Angeles) and in large natural enclosures, including one near Eilat in Israel.

Breeding large numbers of oryx from just a few individuals has inevitably led to genetic problems. Some of the more successful breeding males fathered a disproportionate number of the captive population in the early days. As a result of inbreeding, survival

Arabian oryx *are the palest species of oryx and are superbly adapted to life in the desert. Like other species of oryx, they are characterized by their long, upright horns. They have dark patches on their faces, legs, and at the lower end of the tail.*

rates were low; this problem has been recognized, and careful management of future breeding should ensure that it is overcome with time.

Oryx are now protected and have been adopted as an important symbol of the local culture in the countries to which they have been restored. It is unlikely that the species will die out a second time through carelessness, but the herds remain small, widely scattered, and vulnerable to natural disasters such as disease and drought.

29

Oryx, Scimitar-Horned

Oryx dammah

The scimitar-horned oryx is on the verge of extinction in its native Africa. The expansion of the Sahara Desert has made much of its former range uninhabitable. Fortunately, there are now healthy introduced populations living semiwild in other parts of the world.

The scimitar-horned oryx moves around in small, nomadic groups. The animals may roam over about 40,000 square miles (100,000 sq. km) as they seek out patches of grass that grow in the moisture-retaining valleys between sand dunes. Oryx will travel over 180 miles (300 km) to take advantage of new growth in the valleys after rainfall. This shows the animal's remarkable ability to find its way around. A gathering of over 1,000 animals was reported in 1936, showing that it used to be a numerous species.

The brilliant white coat of the oryx reflects the sun's heat and also helps each animal see the rest of its group from a long way off, even if the herd is spread over a wide area. Unfortunately, their bright coats also make it easy for humans to spot them. In the past trophy hunters used to chase the animals in trucks. More recently, wars and oil have brought guns and wealth to the Sahara, creating a serious threat to wild animals.

Hunting was just one problem facing the oryx. Its northern population became extinct over a century ago, and the southern population has been in retreat for decades.

Survival in the Desert

The scimitar-horned oryx used to live across the northern edge of the Sahara from Morocco in the west to Egypt in the east. Along the southern fringe of the Sahara the species ranged from Mauritania to the Sudan. Its decline suggests that the oryx is facing a widespread and long-term threat, rather than a local or recent problem. Desert rain is scanty and unpredictable at the best of times. It is likely that the oryx has suffered from climatic changes that have caused the rains to fail or to fall elsewhere, leaving areas with insufficient grass to support the small herds. The problem has been made worse by increasing numbers of domestic livestock. Domestic grazing animals compete with wild antelope like the

DATA PANEL

Scimitar-horned oryx

Oryx dammah

Family: Bovidae

World population: Unknown, possibly fewer than 500

Distribution: Formerly widespread, now reintroduced population in southern Tunisia. Large numbers semiwild on game ranches in Texas

Habitat: Hot, dry semidesert, with grassy patches among dunes and scattered acacia trees

Size: Length head/body: 6.6–7.6 ft (1.9–2.2 m); tail: 18–24 in (45–60 cm); height at shoulder: 47–52 in (110–120 cm). Weight: about 300 lb (135 kg), but up to 480 lb (216 kg) in captivity

Form: Pale fawn and white, deep-chested antelope with long, backward-curving horns. Face long; tail long and hairy

Diet: Mostly grass, but also other vegetation, fruit, and seed pods

Breeding: Single calf born after gestation of 7.5–8 months; probably 2 years or more between births in the wild. Life span in captivity more than 17 years

Related endangered species: Arabian oryx (*Oryx leucoryx*)* EN

Status: IUCN EW; CITES I

Balearic Is
Sardinia
ITALY
Sicily
TUNISIA
ALGERIA
LIBYA

See also: Communities and Ecosystems **1:** 22; Captive Breeding **1:** 87; Duiker, Jentink's **4:** 48; Oryx, Arabian **7:** 28

oryx and addax for the limited amount of grass available. In addition, wells sunk into the desert draw up underground water reserves, reducing the amount of water available to support surface vegetation. The sparse vegetation of the desert has also changed: By removing trees for fuel and allowing domestic animals to graze, people have prevented natural regrowth. When plants die, they expose the fine sand and soil to the wind. The soil gets blown around, smothering any remaining vegetation, and preventing photosynthesis (the production of food in plants using sunlight as an energy source). With no vegetation to feed on, wild animals quickly die, and the uninhabitable area of the Sahara has expanded.

In the 1970s there were thought to be about 6,000 oryx surviving along the southern fringe of the Sahara. The few left in a national park in Chad seem now to be extinct. Fortunately, there are at least 1,200 in zoos worldwide. Others live semiwild on game ranches in the southern United States, especially in Texas, and there are also some in Israel, so it is unlikely that the species will die out.

Hopes for the Future

In 1985 some oryx were released in the Bou Hedma Reserve in southern Tunisia. The animals came from zoo stock, but became established in the wild, and numbers have increased to 100 within five years. Along with conservation of the oryx the Tunisian government has committed to protecting the animal's habitat. By imposing limits on domestic livestock, it has encouraged the regeneration of natural vegetation. This recovery means that soil erosion is reduced; the rains no longer cascade off the hills in muddy flows, but are held back and replenish the wells that supply people and their farms. The oryx-conservation project has therefore had widespread benefits.

The scimitar-horned oryx *has long, sharp horns that have rings around them and form an elegant curve like the traditional sword—the scimitar—carried by many desert tribesmen.*

Otter, European

Lutra lutra

The otter has become extinct in many parts of Europe as a result of habitat loss. Now conservation projects are underway, and the remaining populations are recovering.

A widespread and successful species, the otter is found on the banks of rivers and lakes across a huge area of Europe and Russia as far east as China and Japan. It can survive intensely cold winters and feeds on a wide variety of fish and other aquatic animals. In Scotland and parts of Scandinavia otters also live along the seacoast, adjusting their behavior to prey on crabs and mollusks.

For centuries the otter was hunted for sport and for its valuable fur, yet populations were fairly stable. In the 1960s and 1970s otter numbers suddenly dropped, particularly in Britain, but also in the Netherlands, Germany, and other parts of Europe. This was partly as a result of habitat destruction. Turning rivers into canals, engineering projects for flood prevention, and general disturbance (particularly from an increase in angling) all contributed to a reduction in otter numbers. But the prime culprit in the otters' decline was the increasing use of agricultural chemicals, particularly insecticides such as DDT, aldrin, and dieldrin.

Dangerous Chemicals

The use of artificial chemicals on crops and seeds reduces destruction by insects and thereby increases crop yields. However, the toxins take a long time to be eliminated from the environment. When it rains, chemicals are washed off farmland into streams and lakes, where they contaminate the plankton. Fish that feed on the plankton accumulate the toxic residues in their bodies. In turn, an otter eating the affected fish will undergo a buildup of toxic material in its fat and liver. Even if the poisons do not reach lethal levels, the otters might be rendered sterile, and in the 1960s and 1970s this process drove otters into serious decline. As older otters died, there were no young to replace them, and whole populations collapsed.

In countries where agriculture was less intensive, otter populations remained healthy, notably in Portugal, Ireland, Greece, and northern Russia. Otters

DATA PANEL

European otter

Lutra lutra

Family: Mustelidae

World population: At least 10,000

Distribution: Widespread across Europe as far east as China, but in small populations; locally extinct in parts of western Europe

Habitat: River banks and coastal areas

Size: Length head/body: 24–36 in (60–90 cm); tail: 14–18.5 in (36–47 cm); females 10% smaller than males. Weight: males 13.5–37.5 lb (6–17 kg); females 13.5–26.5 lb (6–12 kg)

Form: Long, slim body with short legs, dark-brown coat, and long, tapering tail. Broad muzzle, small eyes and ears. Feet webbed

Diet: Mainly fish (especially eels), but also frogs and occasionally birds. Crayfish and mollusks where abundant

Breeding: Can breed in any month, litters of 2–3 young (up to 5) once a year, or born in alternate years; mature in second year. Life span 3–4 years; increases to 11 in captivity

Related endangered species: European mink (*Mustela lutreola*)* EN; wolverine (*Gulo gulo*)* VU; giant otter (*Pteronura brasiliensis*)* EN

Status: IUCN VU; CITES I

See also: Pesticides **1:** 51; Mink, European **6:** 78; Otter, Giant **7:** 34

living along coasts also largely escaped because they fed on prey that had not been contaminated by agricultural pollutants. The coastal population of Scotland is one of the most successful in western Europe. This group of otters has suffered heavy losses, however, from oil spills and accidents near coastal oil terminals or shipwrecks.

The most dangerous agricultural chemicals are no longer used in most countries, and otter numbers are beginning to increase, spreading back into places where they had died out. However, new threats loom. Acid rain affects many rivers in Europe, leading to a reduction in the numbers of aquatic invertebrates. This leads to fewer fish and less food for the otters, Meanwhile, PCBs—chemicals from industrial sources— pollute many rivers. These accumulate like DDT, but they damage animals at much lower concentrations.

Otters *have smooth fur and a streamlined body. Populations are recovering especially in Finland and in Britain, assisted by reintroductions from captive-bred stock.*

Otter, Giant

Pteronura brasiliensis

Formerly conspicuous and widespread, the giant otter is now extinct in parts of its range. Its decline is mainly a direct result of excessive and uncontrolled hunting.

The giant otter is more sociable than many otter species. It lives in family groups of up to 20 individuals, although most groups are made up of between six to eight animals. There is usually a mated pair, along with their most recently born young, and some offspring from the previous year. Unlike the more familiar river otters of North America and Europe, the group stays close together, and the adult male and female often share the same den.

Giant otters eat what they can get and cooperate with each other when hunting prey by driving shoals of fish into shallow water where they can be caught easily. They use their sensitive whiskers (vibrissae) to detect water turbulence caused by fish and other potential prey and pursue their victim underwater, catching it in their jaws. Otters often take slow-moving species, such as catfish, and will eat fish over 2 feet (60 cm) long. They wait for their partners to finish eating before moving on.

When ashore, giant otters mark out their riverbank territory with scent. One consequence of this is that it sends out a warning to other individuals or families in the area. Giant otters are also vocal, calling to each other with a wide range of squeals, barks, and whistles. Although useful for communication, such announcements make it easy for human hunters to locate and kill family groups.

Unlike many other mustelids, which are active under cover of darkness, giant otters are mainly active during the day. Coming out in daylight hours exposes the animals to many dangers, particularly from hunters with spears or guns. Another potentially fatal behavioral trait is the otter's curiosity. The animals swim around with their heads held high out of the water and will often move toward intruders, or possibly dangerous situations, to investigate them more closely. Again, such behavior makes them easy prey, and hunters are usually able to kill others of the group who linger to see what has happened.

Hunted for Fur

As in other species of otter, the fur of the giant otter is extremely dense and helps protect the animal from getting chilled when in the water. The giant otter's fur is particularly distinctive, being short, glossy, and velvety. Such qualities make it especially attractive as a fashion fur. Often a hunter will be able to sell a skin for the equivalent of two to three month's honest wages. After processing, the skin is worth five times as much to the fur trade. Official figures from Peru show that every year in the 1950s, over 1,000 giant otter skins were exported; numbers fell sharply as the giant otter population collapsed, and the trade in their pelts

See also: Luxury Products 1: 46; Otter, European 7: 32

and other parts was finally banned in 1970. However, it is thought likely that poaching continues, with skins being sent for export through neighboring countries such as Colombia.

The opening up of huge areas of South American forest for logging has made previously remote otter retreats more accessible to developers and others. Although the species was formerly widespread throughout tropical South America, giant otters are now extinct or nearly so in Argentina, Uruguay, and much of southern Brazil, and they have gone from many other parts of their former range. Recovery of the population is no easy task since the animal's main food—the fish in the river—is in demand to feed people as well, and there are increasing problems of pollution. A particular problem is chemical pollution from gold extraction along rivers. Settlements along river banks also make it difficult for the otters to find undisturbed places for dens.

The giant otter *is the largest of the freshwater otter species, with a distinctive flattened tail. It is still fairly numerous in the Pantanal and in parts of Peru.*

DATA PANEL

Giant otter

Pteronura brasiliensis

Family: Mustelidae

World population: Unknown, possibly 1,000–2,000

Distribution: Formerly found over much of tropical South America, south to Argentina. Probably extinct in Argentina and most of Paraguay

Habitat: Slow-moving rivers, creeks, and swamps within forested areas

Size: Length head/body: 36–58 in (86–140 cm); tail: 14–42 in (33–100 cm). Weight: males 57–75 lb (26–34 kg); females 48–57 lb (22–26 kg)

Form: Large otter with short, glossy-brown fur that appears black when wet. Often white or creamy nose and throat. Feet webbed; tail tapering and flattened with a flange along each edge

Diet: Mainly fish; also freshwater crabs and occasionally mammals

Breeding: Up to 5 young in a single litter per year, born after gestation of 65–70 days. Life span over 14 years in captivity

Related endangered species: Marine otter (*Lutra felina*) EN; smooth-coated otter (*L. perspicillata*) VU; southern river otter (*L. provocax*) EN; hairy-nosed otter (*L. sumatrana*) DD; European otter (*L. lutra*)* VU

Status: IUCN EN; CITES I

Otter, Sea

Enhydra lutris

Excessive hunting lead to the extermination of the sea otter from most of its range along north Pacific coasts. It recovered to about half its previous population levels through international protection, but is declining again.

The sea otter is one of the few mammals that uses tools: It employs a stone to smash open crabs, sea urchins, and mollusks caught on its shallow dives to the seabed. Intelligent animals, sea otters have learned to rip open sunken, discarded drink cans in which a small octopus may hide. Sea otters are important ecologically since they control the numbers of sea urchins, which eat a lot of growing kelp. Exposed coasts are protected against heavy wave action by the kelp beds. Where sea otter numbers have declined, urchins have increased and prevented proper growth of the floating kelp beds.

Sea otters are generally solitary animals, although they sometimes gather in groups. They are exclusively marine and usually fairly sedentary, but some occasionally go on long journeys, of about 100 miles (160 km) along the coast.

The sea otter lives in the cold waters of the north Pacific and spends a lot of time floating at the surface, grooming, or sleeping among the kelp beds. It is one of the smallest sea mammals and needs very effective insulation to reduce loss of body heat. Its fur is the densest known, with more than 600,000 hairs per square inch (93,000 per sq. cm)—twice the density of a fur seal's coat.

For centuries the thick pelt was highly valued, and the sea otter was ruthlessly hunted off the coasts of Kamchatka in Russia and in the eastern Pacific. Explorations by 18th-century navigators expanded the trade in skins, and colonization of Alaska by the Russians intensified the pressures on the species across the north Pacific. The skins became the world's most valuable fur, each pelt worth the equivalent of a seaman's wages for an

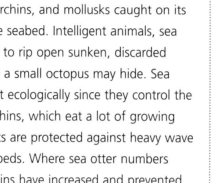

DATA PANEL

Sea otter

Enhydra lutris

Family: Mustelidae

World population: About 15,000 (1999)

Distribution: Coasts of California, eastern Russia (Kamchatka and Commander Islands). Successfully reintroduced to coasts of Alaska, Oregon, and Washington

Habitat: Rocky coasts and kelp beds

Size: Length head/body: 30–36 in (75–90 cm); tail: 11–13 in (28–32 cm); height at shoulder: 8–10 in (20–25 cm). Weight: 30–85 lb (14–40 kg)

Form: Dark-brown coat with a cream, blunt-looking head. The feet are completely webbed, the hind ones forming flippers

Diet: Crabs, shellfish, sea-urchins, fish, and other marine animals; about 13 lb (6 kg) daily

Breeding: Breeds all year round, but most births occur in early summer. Only 1 pup is born each year. Life span can exceed 20 years

Related endangered species: Giant otter (*Pteronura brasiliensis*)* EN; European mink (*Mustela lutreola*)* EN

Status: IUCN EN; CITES II

See also: Hunting **1:** 42; Pollution **1:** 50; Otter, European **7:** 32; Otter, Giant **7:** 34

entire year. Records show that over 750,000 sea otters were killed between 1750 and 1850, and that a single shipment of 17,000 skins was made in 1803.

Sea otters were easily hunted from kayaks; hunters chased the animals until they were too breathless to dive, then speared them. Each body would be skinned in the kayak and the next otter sought out. Living along the coast, and with no safety at sea, the otters could be hunted until every last one had been caught.

Success Story

Sea otters do not breed rapidly, so they became extinct over wide areas. In 1911 the Russians, Americans, and British (on behalf of Canada) agreed on total protection for the sea otter throughout the north Pacific. Gradually numbers have increased, and they are appearing again in many of their former

A sea otter *floats on its back. In such a position the animal can open a mollusk shell, crab, or sea-urchin by smashing it against a stone balanced on its chest.*

habitats. It was thought that sea otters were extinct on the California coast, but in 1938 a few were found. Numbers have grown to more than 2,000. In fact, fishermen now complain that there are too many. Animals have been transported to Washington state, Oregon, and Alaska, successfully repopulating those coasts; reintroductions to the Pribilof Islands off Alaska appear to have been less successful.

The sea otter, having been reduced to fewer than 1,000 animals in the whole North Pacific, seems to have made a comeback. However, the otters still face a variety of threats—some of them natural, such as the risk of predation by killer whales. Others are man-made and include oil spills and other pollution.

Owl, Blakiston's Eagle

Bubo blakistoni

The magnificent Blakiston's eagle owl has undergone a tragic and devastating decline due entirely to human impact, ranging from forest destruction and overfishing to persecution by hunters. Today it is one of the world's rarest owls.

Blakiston's eagle owl is an imposing bird, the largest of all the world's owls, with a wingspan of over 6 feet (1.8 m). It has two tufts of head feathers and large, orange-yellow eyes. Although it has been classified with the fish owls, recent research suggests that it is an unusual member of the eagle owl group, which includes the more numerous and widespread northern eagle owl, found from western Europe all across Asia to eastern Siberia. The growing human effect on its already difficult habitat, especially acute over the last 50 years, threatens to push the bird toward extinction unless serious efforts are made to reverse the trend.

Rare throughout its range, the Blakiston's eagle owl is a bird of dense, dark primeval forests bordering rivers, streams, and lakes in remote areas of northeastern Asia,

where the winters are bitterly cold. Here it feeds mainly on fish—including large salmon, pike, catfish, and burbot—but it also preys on frogs, insects, crayfish, birds, and small mammals. The owls live as pairs and stay on the same territory for life. They do not breed until they are at least three years old and are usually unable to rear more than one young every other year.

The owls prefer to live along fast-flowing rivers and streams or by deep springs, where the water does not normally freeze. In severe winters, however, the water may be locked in the grip of ice. During such hard times small groups have been seen together at productive sites, where air holes remain in the ice—but only in areas where enough of the owls remain. The principal threats facing Blakiston's eagle owl are the logging of forests and the development of land along riverbanks, together with the conversion of

DATA PANEL

Blakiston's eagle owl (Blakiston's fish owl)

Bubo blakistoni

Family: Strigidae

World population: Total about 400–1,800 birds: Russian population estimated at a few hundred to 1,600; up to 100 in China; estimated 120 birds on Hokkaido

Distribution: Southeastern Russia, including the island of Sakhalin and adjacent parts of China. Also found in Hokkaido Island, Japan, and the southern Kuril Islands belonging to Russia

Habitat: Densely wooded lowland river valleys; also hunts on rocky sea coasts

Size: Length: 24–28 in (60–72 cm); wingspan: 6–6.3 ft (1.8–1.9 m)

Form: Massive body with buff-brown upperparts; pale-buff underparts with long, narrow streaks. Long, horizontal ear tufts; gray-brown face; buff and dark-brown barred wings; whitish tail with dark bars; legs feathered to base of toes

Diet: Fish; also frogs, crayfish, crabs, and other crustaceans; birds up to size of grouse; small mammals, including bats taken in flight

Breeding: Lays 1–3 (usually 2) off-white eggs February–March, in hole in a hollow tree up to 60 ft (18 m) above ground. Sometimes uses a fallen tree or the ground; also nest boxes. Eggs incubated by female for about 5 weeks; young leave nest at 5–6 weeks and may depend on parents for up to a year. Usually breeds only every 2 years

Related endangered species: Philippine eagle owl (*Bubo philippensis*) VU; spot-bellied eagle owl (*B. nipalensis*) LRnt; Usambara eagle owl (*B. vosseleri*) VU; rufous fishing owl (*Scotopelia ussheri*) EN

Status: IUCN EN; CITES II

See also: Populations 1: 20; Owl, Madagascar Red 7: 40; Owl, Spotted 7: 42

forest to farmland, and the building of dams. Other threats include the overharvesting of fish, especially salmon and their relatives. Hunters in Russia kill an unknown number of the owls, and some also die in traps set for mink by fur trappers, who regard them unfairly as competitors for their quarry. In parts of Siberia they are even hunted for food.

Owls on Hokkaido

Blakiston's eagle owl could once be found throughout Hokkaido, the second largest of the islands of Japan. Today it has been pushed back to remoter parts of the east and center, especially Shiretoko National Park. The Ainu people (themselves a remnant of their former population) regarded the giant owl with reverence, referring to it as "the god who defends the villages." However, despite being declared a national treasure by the Japanese government in 1971, today only about 120 birds survive there, and they suffer from many human threats.

Although the island was not settled by the Japanese until the late 19th century, little of Hokkaido's native forest remains, most having been felled or converted to plantations of introduced conifers. Overfishing and the building of dams reduce the owls' food supply. The birds are also killed in collisions with powerlines and road traffic, and drown in nets on fish farms. It is estimated that 25 percent of the birds on Hokkaido survive only because they are artificially fed, and 40 percent of the pairs breeding there can do so only because conservationists provide them with nest boxes.

Blakiston's eagle owl, *one of the rarest of its group, has two tufts of feathers on the head.*

Owl, Madagascar Red

Tyto soumagnei

Until recently the enigmatic Madagascar red owl was one of the world's least-known birds. New research is revealing some of the secrets of its life, and there is hope that it may not be quite as rare as was once feared.

The beautiful Madagascar red owl was first discovered by ornithologists in 1876. It was initially considered rare—although the small number of sightings may have been partly related to the inhospitable nature of its rainforest habitat and its strictly nocturnal habits.

Until recently there had been only one confirmed sighting of the owl (in 1973) since the last specimen was collected in 1934. Given the alarming rate of forest destruction on the island, the bird was thought to be extremely rare. However, during the 1990s a number of the owls were seen in six different sites in the eastern rainforest zone, ranging from Amber Mountain in the far north to Mantadia National Park in the center of eastern Madagascar. Indeed, the owls probably occur in all the remaining blocks of forest in the northeast of the island that are large enough to support a population.

An intensive program of fieldwork in the 1990s resulted in ornithologists trapping a Madagascar red owl in October 1994 and fitting it with a radio transmitting collar. This enabled the researchers to monitor its movements and to fill at least some gaps in their knowledge of the species, which up until then was almost nonexistent.

In September 1995 the radio-tagged owl nested and raised two young. This was the first recorded nest of the species. It was sited 75 feet (23 m) above ground in a natural hollow within an isolated tree of a native species, *Weinmannia*, 1,650 feet (500 m) from the edge of the main area of forest.

As well as providing information about their breeding behavior, observations and radio tracking by researchers at the study site revealed that the owls hunt in open areas or along the edge of the forest. There are occasional records of red owls catching rats and old accounts of them eating frogs; but they are specialists, preying almost exclusively on small native

DATA PANEL

Madagascar red owl (Madagascar grass owl)

Tyto soumagnei

Family: Tytonidae

World population: About 1,000–2,500 birds

Distribution: Madagascar: several sites in the eastern rain forests; probably occurs in other forest in the east and north of the island

Habitat: Primary evergreen rain forest; also human-altered, forest-edge habitats

Size: Length: 11–12 in (27.5–30 cm). Weight: about 11.3 oz (320 g)

Form: Medium-sized owl, similar to barn owl but smaller; orange-red plumage, dark above and pale below; facial disk tinged gray-buff, darker round black eyes and fringed with orange; crown, upperparts, and underparts speckled with black dots; tail faintly barred. Juveniles similar to adults, but brighter at first

Diet: Mainly small native mammals; also the occasional rat and possibly frogs

Breeding: Only recorded nest 75 ft (23 m) above ground in natural tree hollow; probably 2 eggs in a clutch (in radio-tagged owl 2 young fledged at 10 weeks); young stay in area of nest for at least 4 months

Related endangered species: Congo bay owl (*Phodilus prigoginei*) EN; Minahasa masked owl (*Tyto inexspectata*) VU; Taliabu masked owl (*T. nigrobrunnea*) EN; 3 other species of masked owls classified as DD

Status: IUCN EN; CITES I and II

See also: Habitat Loss **1:** 38; National Parks **1:** 92; Owl, Blakiston's Eagle **7:** 38; Owl, Spotted **7:** 42

mammals, particularly shrewlike and molelike animals of the native tenrec family and tuft-tailed rats.

Although the species was thought to be restricted to undisturbed primary rain forest at altitudes of between 3,000 and 3,900 feet (900 and 1,200 m), recent studies of red owls suggest that rice paddies and other open cultivated areas may be important for hunting. Some birds have been found roosting in small ravines among plantations of bananas and secondary growth forest.

Forest Destruction

Along with a great range of other native plants and animals, the Madagascar red owl faces severe threats from the continued destruction of its main rainforest habitat. Almost all of Madagascar's native species have an uncertain future due to the massive scale of natural habitat destruction that has occurred on the island over a long period of human colonization. A great proportion of the eastern forests has been cleared for subsistence slash-and-burn cultivation and in some areas has been replaced with plantations of exotic, fast-growing pine and eucalyptus trees that are unsuitable for the Madagascar red owl.

The loss of forests also affects the owl's native mammal prey and thus the owl itself—as well as lemurs and many other birds, including the Critically Endangered Madagascar serpent eagle, the Endangered yellow-bellied asity, and three Vulnerable species of ground rollers; none of the birds is found anywhere else in the world. In total an astonishing 89 percent of Madagascar's threatened birds occur nowhere else on earth.

Finding More Owls

Targets for conservationists include surveys to the south of the owl's known range to determine whether the bird occurs there or not. A census of populations is also planned. Recordings of the owl's calls will be played to encourage it to reply, so its presence can be confirmed and numbers counted.

It is hoped that such investigations will show that the Madagascar red owl is less rare than it is presently feared to be. Each of the six sites where it has been recorded recently is identified as an Important Bird Area. They include protected areas such as Mantadia National Park, Marotandrano Special Reserve, and Tsaratanana Strict Reserve. The protection provided by national parks and other reserves remains the best hope for the species' survival.

The Madagascar red owl—*found only on the island of Madagascar—prefers to live in undisturbed humid rain forests.*

41

Owl, Spotted

Strix occidentalis

Largely restricted to the ancient conifer and oak forests that once extended all along the Pacific coast of North America, the spotted owl is being driven from its ancestral habitats by logging operations that target the biggest, oldest, and most valuable trees.

Found in four distinct populations from southwestern Canada to Mexico, the spotted owl is primarily a bird of mature, moist, temperate forests. Throughout its range it is a night hunter that uses its acute hearing and night-adapted eyesight to pinpoint small mammals and birds in the darkness as it perches above the forest floor. Swooping down on silent wings, it seizes its victim in its feathered talons and returns to the perch to sever its spinal cord with its bill. Then it swallows the prey whole, headfirst.

The forests of great redwoods, pines, hemlocks, cedars, and oaks provide the spotted owl with a wealth of prey and plenty of quiet roosting sites where it can spend the day undisturbed.

They also offer ideal nesting holes in big, mature trees, although the owl will sometimes use a rock cavity or even an abandoned squirrel nest. Many spotted owls stay on their nesting territories throughout the year, defending them against trespassing rivals with loud whoops and shrieks that echo through the forest. It is an eerie, evocative, and increasingly rare sound.

Logged Out

As is the case elsewhere, ancient forests of western North America are being destroyed for their timber. Secondary forest is no replacement for the rich, multilayered patchwork of trees, shrubs, and undergrowth that develops naturally over the centuries. It does not have the same diversity of wildlife—which for the spotted owl means prey—and the young trees lack holes and snags where birds can

DATA PANEL

Spotted owl

Strix occidentalis

Family: Strigidae

World population: About 15,000 birds in 4 races

Distribution: Western North America: northern race *S. o. caurina* from southern British Columbia to northern California; California race *S. o. occidentalis* through central and southern California; Mexican race *S. o. lucida* scattered from southern Utah to central Mexico; the fourth, from the State of Mexico in southern central Mexico, recently described and named *juanaphillipsae*

Habitat: Mainly moist, temperate old-growth conifer or oak forest, but Mexican race also occurs in warmer, drier, secondary pine-oak forest and rocky canyons

Size: Length: 16–19 in (41–48 cm). Weight: 1.1–1.7 lb (520–760 g)

Form: Medium-sized, upright, round-headed owl with well-defined facial disk, black eyes, and fully feathered feet. Upperparts rich red-brown, with white spots on head and neck; mottled buff on back and wings; underparts barred whitish and rust-brown. Mexican race paler. Juvenile pale brown with dark barring

Diet: Mainly small mammals; also roosting birds (including small owls) and insects

Breeding: Birds pair for life, nesting March–June. Usually 2 eggs, laid on bare floor of tree cavity or crevice and incubated by female for 30 days. Downy chicks brooded by female for 2 weeks while male brings food, then both parents forage; fledged young leave nest at 35 days

Related endangered species: Twenty-three other owls in the family Strigidae, including Blakiston's eagle owl (*Bubo blakistoni*)* EN; São Tomé scops-owl (*Otus hartlaubi*) VU; Sokoke scops-owl (*O. ireneae*) EN; rufous fishing-owl (*Scotopelia ussheri*) EN; and long-whiskered owlet (*Xenoglaux loweryi*) EN

Status: IUCN LRnt; CITES II

See also: Categories of Threat 1: 14; Habitat Loss 1: 38; Owl, Blakiston's Eagle 7: 38; Owl, Madagascar Red 7: 40

nest and perch. Spotted owls avoid plantations that are fewer than 100 years old, and a forest has to be at least 200 years old for it to become suitable breeding habitat.

The old trees are the biggest and most valuable. Consequently, tracts of prime old-growth forest have been clear-felled, leaving nothing but stumps. Where big trees are more scattered, they are often selectively felled to leave younger, smaller trees. Both strategies are catastrophic for the owl, especially the northern race. It is estimated that in the northwestern United States the degree of spotted owl habitat loss ranges from 54 percent to over 99 percent.

Logging and the spread of farmland and towns, reservoir development, and mining have led to a steep decline in the population of spotted owls. There are some 8,500 of the northern race surviving in the huge swath of coastal forest from Canada to northern California. The California race is in trouble too, with about 3,000 left. The more adaptable Mexican race numbers up to 1,500 in the American part of its range, with perhaps 2,000 in Mexico itself; the southern owls seem to be holding their own, partly because they are less tied to old-growth forest, but also because they are not suffering such heavy habitat losses.

The spotted owl is classified as Lower Risk, near threatened rather than Endangered, but its decline is accelerating, and it has become the subject of six management plans in Canada and the United States. It has also been the focus of a heated debate between conservationists, timber companies, and politicians over the future of the forests.

The spotted owl, *like many other nocturnal owl species, has a facial disk that helps reflect sound to the ears, helping the birds locate prey.*

Ox, Vu Quang

Pseudoryx nghetinhensis

In spite of its considerable size, the Vu Quang ox was only recently discovered. One reason for its obscurity was its remote forest habitat. Today, however, even the most secluded parts of its range are at risk from development.

The Vu Quang ox is the size of a small pony. It is rare for such a big mammal to escape the notice of science. However, the Vu Quang ox only came to the attention of the outside world in 1992, when some horns were found by hunters in the Vu Quang Reserve on the border between Vietnam and Laos. The reserve lies in an area of extensive, steeply sloping forests that are apparently the ox's main home. Enquiries among local people suggested that it could be found widely in the forests, but also that it was already uncommon and becoming more so. The local name for the ox—"sao la," meaning "spindle horn"—is a reference to the animal's sharp horns, which supposedly resemble needles used in weaving. Their straight, backward-sloping form suggests that the ox may be related to the oryx, and the similarity is referred to in the animal's scientific name of *Pseudoryx*. However, the ox also shares characteristics with the serow (a kind of Asian goat), the anoa, and even some African antelopes.

Local hunters kill the oxen for their meat, although recently they have been eager to obtain live specimens for scientists to study. A female captured in 1996 proved surprisingly tame; it spent much of its time in captivity resting with its chin and neck on the ground. It also used prominent scent glands on its face to mark parts of its enclosure, a behavior probably also found in the wild, where the animals have to keep track of each other in the dense, dark forest. The captive animal was mainly active during the day, although in the wild the creatures are probably largely nocturnal.

Forest Range

Wild Vu Quang oxen live alone or in pairs; sometimes a female may be seen with her young. Females probably produce only a single offspring, according to local hunters usually in February or March, before the main rainy season begins. The animals' habitat consists of dense evergreen or semideciduous forest on steep mountain slopes cut by deep valleys. The oxen live at up to 6,500 feet (2,000 m) above sea level in summer, although they are said to descend to

---

DATA PANEL

Vu Quang ox (sao la)

Pseudoryx nghetinhensis

Family: Bovidae

World population: Unknown, probably only a few hundred at most

Distribution: Laos, Vietnam

Habitat: Dense mountain forests, moving to lower altitudes during the dry winter months

Size: Length head/body: 5–6.7 ft (1.5–2 m); tail: 5 in (13 cm); height at shoulder: 2.7–3 ft (80–90 cm). Weight: 200 lb (90 kg)

Form: Dark-brown antelopelike animal with white "socks," white eyebrows, and spots on the face, chin, and nose. Brown tail with cream band and black tip. Prominent scent gland forms a slit in front of each eye. Both sexes have thin horns that curve slightly backward and are up to 20 in (50 cm) long

Diet: Leaves browsed from low shrubs; grass

Breeding: Probably only 1 young born per year in February or March after gestation of about 8 months. Life span unknown

Related endangered species: Saiga *(Saiga tatarica)** LRcd; various other antelopes and oryxes

Status: IUCN EN; CITES I

See also: Research **1:** 84; Banteng **2:** 50; Kouprey **6:** 14

lower altitudes in the drier months of winter, the season when they are most at risk of capture. The animal's forest home stretches over an area of at least 1,500 square miles (4,000 sq. km), spanning the border between Laos and Vietnam. It includes areas specially protected by the governments of both countries, which have now been extended to accommodate the Vu Quang ox. In theory the animal should be safe in such secluded forests, but in practice it is often difficult to protect wildlife in remote areas. Hunting has continued, even during the 1990s, when the newly discovered animals were the focus of much conservation attention.

The ox owes its survival to date largely to the inaccessibility of the region. There are few roads, and the steep terrain has proved unattractive to settlers, not least because of the almost continuous wars that have plagued Vietnam for more than half a century. In such circumstances few people chose to exploit the forest, and those that did risked being killed.

The resulting lack of development has prevented the usual conflicts that arise between the needs of wild mammals and the demands of expanding farms and towns. It has also meant that the forests have remained untouched by loggers, and there is consequently the exciting possibility that other new species lurk there and in similar forests in Cambodia.

Increased exploration brings new risks. Now that peace has come to the region, the pressures from farming and logging are set to increase. Steep mountains with heavy rainfall are also ideal sites for hydroelectric projects that bring roads, industry, and people in their wake. The Vu Quang ox has come to the attention of the outside world only to join the growing list of endangered species.

The Vu Quang ox *resembles various other animals such as the oryx, but its true classification and ecology are still not precisely known.*

Paddlefish

Polyodon spathula

The paddlefish, with its distinctive, paddlelike snout, is one of the strangest-looking fish in the world. It is also a source of caviar—the expensive delicacy made from salted roe (eggs), usually of the sturgeon fish.

The paddlefish is a substantial animal with an equally substantial appetite. Like other large predators such as the whale shark and its relative, the basking shark, it does not hunt down and kill large prey. Instead, it feeds by swimming through "clouds" of plankton with its mouth open, straining out the tiny organisms with its sievelike gill rakers.

Paddle Purpose

The paddle (rostrum, or beaklike part) of the fish accounts for almost a third of its body length, and its exact function is still a mystery. It has long been thought to play a fundamentally important role during feeding, and some experts believe it to be a tool that the fish uses to stir up the mud. That is probably not the case since the paddlefish's main food source is freeswimming microscopic invertebrates. It is more likely that the rich supply of sensory cells in the paddle helps the fish detect and locate its food. It could also act as a stabilizer when the fish swims with its cavernous mouth open. However, it has been noted that when a paddlefish has lost part or the whole of the paddle through injury, it can still detect food and feed adequately.

Ancient Relationships

Fossil evidence shows that paddlefish have existed since the the Cretaceous and Eocene periods (about 135 million years ago) when dinosaurs existed. Like the primitive marine bony fish the coelacanth, they are regarded as "living fossils." The paddlefish's long operculi (gill covers) are probably a primitive feature.

Paddlefish have a skeleton made of cartilage (a tough, elastic tissue), like sharks, although the jaw is made of bone. The caudal (tail) fin is also sharklike, having a long top lobe. The skin is virtually scaleless

CANADA

UNITED STATES

MEXICO   CUBA

DATA PANEL

American paddlefish (duckbill cat, shovelfish, spadefish, spoonbill)

Polyodon spathula

Family: Polyodontidae

World population: Unknown—relatively abundant in traditional waters; scarce or absent in others

Distribution: Mainly Mississippi River Basin and Gulf Slope drainage, U.S.

Habitat: Slow-flowing waters; prefer oxbow lakes and backwaters where the depth exceeds about 4 ft (1.2 m)

Size: Length: up to 6.6 ft (2 m). Mature females larger than males. Weight: over 100 lb (45 kg)

Form: Elongated body; sharklike with rostrum (paddlelike snout). Slate colored, often mottled, with lighter shading in the lower half

Diet: Small invertebrates (zooplankton) and insect larvae

Breeding: Spawning in April and May at water temperatures of about 55°F (13°C). Females can produce about 7,500 eggs per 1 lb (450 g) of body weight. The large eggs hatch in about a week and the fry are free-swimming. Juveniles grow at a rate of 1 in (2.5 cm) per week. Females mature at 10 years. Life span 30 years

Related endangered species: Chinese paddlefish *(Psephurus gladius)* CR

Status: IUCN VU; CITES II

See also: Luxury Products 1: 46; Special Techniques 1: 88; Sturgeon, Common 9: 36

and the jaws toothless, although young specimens have numerous tiny teeth that they gradually lose as they mature. Young are born without a paddle.

Today paddlefish have few living relatives; the closest are the 25 species of sturgeon, with which they share the order Acipenseriformes.

Threats to Survival

Paddlefish were once common in their native waters, but habitat alteration, reduced water quality, and overfishing all led to a significant decrease in numbers.

Habitat alteration has been of two major types: watercourse channelization and dam building. Both have deprived the paddlefish of essential feeding and spawning areas. Water degradation has occurred primarily as a result of pollution, while overfishing has been largely illegal and relatively recent.

Stocks are now on the increase in some parts of the species' original range. However, a sharp decline in paddlefish numbers occurred as a result of overfishing during the 1980s, when sturgeon from Iran were unavailable—Iran was fighting a war. Paddlefish were then poached to make up the shortfall.

The American paddlefish *is greenish gray and inhabits the Mississippi Basin. The other species, the larger Chinese paddlefish, inhabits the Yangtse River Basin.*

Conserving Stocks

Where the paddlefish is fairly abundant, it is fished on a strict quota basis; it is hoped that this will lead to sustainable natural stocks. In many inland waters, as well as the paddlefish's traditional stronghold, the Mississippi River, fishing continues all year round but only allows a maximum catch of two fish per day. On the Missouri River there is no open season.

Running alongside such measures, a number of hatchery-based programs—set up in the early 1990s—produced thousands of juveniles for restocking. Tagging of many of the hatchery-raised juveniles is leading to greater understanding of the species. It will, however, be several years before we know how successful these fish are at reproducing in the wild.

Panda, Giant

Ailuropoda melanoleuca

Adopted as the emblem of the Worldwide Fund for Nature and popular the world over, the giant panda has come to symbolize endangered animals and efforts to save them.

T he giant panda is probably one of the most distinctive and instantly recognizable animals in the world, yet probably fewer than 100 have ever been seen alive outside China. Traditionally, pandas were associated with magical properties. As a result, they have been killed for their skins and body parts. Many have also been caught accidentally in snares set for the valuable musk deer.

Pandas breed very slowly: Females are fertile for only two to three days in the year. The young take over a year to reach independence and do not breed until they are at least five years old.

The giant panda is found in cool, damp, mountain bamboo forests. An individual may spend most of its time within a single square mile of a valley or mountain ridge in which it must find all the food it needs. The animals are specialized feeders. Although they will eat roots and even mice, their main diet is bamboo. Since bamboo is not very nutritious, the panda needs a great deal of it and must spend 10 hours a day feeding. It has a bony extension of the wrist—a kind of thumb—that helps it grip bamboo shoots firmly.

By the time winter arrives, supplies of bamboo in the panda's territory are running out. As temperatures drop, the animals need even more food to maintain their body heat, so they move to lower altitudes in search of more abundant growth. Such a migration is possible only so long as the main areas of panda habitat are intact. However, at lower altitudes mountain forests are being increasingly carved up for farmland; logging is also destroying the panda's forest

The giant panda, *with its stubby tail and distinctive black-and-white markings, has always been popular in zoos. Captive-breeding attempts have attracted media attention, and the species probably owes its survival to its high profile.*

habitat. Sichuan Province, the panda's main home, has lost a third of its forest in 30 years, leaving the animals isolated in small, inaccessible patches. Another problem for the giant panda is the increase in human population and settlement in lowland areas: The animals are left stranded at higher elevations.

Threats and Solutions

The contraction of bamboo habitat presents a serious threat to the giant panda. The situation is made worse by the bamboo's peculiar habit of flowering every so often and then dying, a phenomenon that appears to be on the increase as a result of long-term climate change. It takes several years for a new crop to grow. Periodically, the panda's main food supply simply dies out over large areas. In the 1970s, when three species of bamboo flowered at once and then died, over 100 pandas (more than a tenth of the entire population) are known to have starved to death.

Nowadays the population is fairly stable, although perilously small and fragmented. Attempts at captive breeding have not been very successful; a few young have been born, but their survival rate is low. Protection of the species and its habitat appears to be the most effective way to save the giant panda from extinction. Special sanctuaries have now been created, and the animal is well protected under Chinese law.

See also: Organizations **1:** 10; Specialization **1:** 28; Bear, Sloth **2:** 72; Bear, Spectacled **2:** 74; Panda, Lesser **7:** 50

DATA PANEL

Giant panda

Ailuropoda melanoleuca

Family: Ursidae (sometimes considered one of the Procyonidae, or assigned its own family, the Ailuridae)

World population: About 1,000

Distribution: Central provinces of China

Habitat: Mountain bamboo forests up to 12,800 ft (3,900 m) above sea level

Size: Length head/body: 4–5 ft (1.2–1.5 m); tail: about 5 in (12–13 cm); height at shoulder: about 24 in (60 cm). Weight: 165–350 lb (75–160 kg)

Form: Stocky, bearlike animal with creamy-white fur; black legs, shoulders, ears, eye patches, and nose

Diet: Mainly bamboo; also bulbs and other plant materials; occasionally fish and small animals

Breeding: Up to 3 young born at a time, but normally only 1 is reared successfully. Pandas take more than 5 years to reach maturity and may not breed every year. Life span in captivity up to 34 years, probably much less in the wild

Related endangered species: Lesser panda *(Ailurus fulgens)** EN

Status: IUCN EN; CITES II

Panda, Lesser

Ailurus fulgens

For about 50 years the lesser, or red, panda was the only known species of panda. Now the animal is experiencing many of the same problems as its more famous relative, the giant panda.

The lesser, or red, panda lives in Himalayan forests at altitudes of between 6,500 and 15,750 feet (2,000 and 4,800 m). Slightly bigger than a domestic cat, it has thick, reddish-brown fur on most of its body, while the long tail is marked with conspicuous red and beige bands. Lesser pandas are excellent climbers, capable of scampering up and down trees headfirst. The tail is not prehensile (adapted for seizing or grasping), but nevertheless it makes an effective counterbalance. Lesser pandas have a waddling gait when moving on the ground, due to the fact that their front legs are angled inward.

Like the giant panda, the lesser panda has an unusual thumb. In its ancestors the thumb was reduced to a mere claw; but when the animal began to adapt to a vegetarian diet, the ability to grip foliage became an advantage. Instead of replacing the thumb, however, natural selection favored a different arrangement; a small bone in the panda's wrist, called the radial sesamoid, enlarged to provide a substitute structure that the panda now uses to grasp food.

Although the panda is almost entirely herbivorous, its digestive system resembles that of a carnivore, with a simple stomach and a short gut. Most herbivores have long intestines to provide the digestive efficiency necessary to cope with their tough, fibrous food. The lesser panda's gut is not well adapted to a diet of plant material, so much of the nutritional value of the food it consumes is wasted. Pandas therefore have to eat more than other herbivores of similar size, and their metabolism is generally sluggish to help conserve energy. Unlike giant pandas, however, lesser pandas are not restricted to a bamboo diet; they also eat the leaves, flowers, fruit, roots, and bark of other plants, and have been known to eat fungi and even insects, birds' eggs, and occasionally nestlings.

Lesser pandas mate early in the winter, and the young are born about 19 weeks later. Heavily pregnant females prepare for the births by furnishing a secure nest site, often in a tree hole or rocky crevice, with twigs, leaves, and grass. Here they have litters of between one and four cubs, which they tend more or less continuously for about a week. After that the mother spends increasingly long periods out of the nest foraging, but she returns regularly to suckle and clean her family, whom she recognizes individually by smell. This pattern continues for about three months until the young cubs are ready to leave the nest. To begin with, they do so only under the cover of darkness, and they stay very close to their mother.

The family will stay together for a short while longer, until the breeding season comes around again, and the mother drives the youngsters away. They then take up solitary lives and have little contact with other pandas. When two animals do meet, they may engage in a variety of raccoonlike displays, including back-arching, head-shaking, jaw-snapping, and standing up on two legs. If they survive to adulthood, the young pandas will be ready to breed themselves the following year, at about 18 months of age.

Puzzles and Problems

There is an ongoing debate as to whether the pandas belong in the bear family (Ursidae) or with the raccoons (Procyonidae). The lesser panda's DNA is bearlike, but its overall body shape is closer to that of a raccoon. Many authorities now place the pandas in a family of their own—the Ailuridae.

See also: Specialization **1:** 28; War **1:** 47; Deer, Siberian Musk **4:** 12; Panda, Giant **7:** 48

DATA PANEL

Lesser panda (red panda)

Ailurus fulgens

Family: Ursidae (sometimes placed in the raccoon family Procyonidae, or assigned its own family, the Ailuridae)

World population: Unknown, but unlikely to exceed a few thousand

Distribution: Himalayan regions of Nepal, Bhutan, Myanmar (Burma), and China (Sichuan and Yunnan provinces)

Habitat: Forest at altitudes of 6,500–15,750 ft (2,000–4,800 m)

Size: Length head/body: 19–23 in (50–60 cm); tail: 12–20 in (30–51 cm). Weight: 6–13 lb (3–6 kg)

Form: Tree-dwelling, racoonlike animal, the size of a large domestic cat. Rich, chestnut-colored fur, darker on belly; tail is banded chestnut and beige; face attractively marked in beige and white

Diet: Berries, blossoms, birds' eggs, leaves of various plants, especially bamboo; also roots, vegetables, fruit, small birds, and mammals

Breeding: Between 1 and 4 young born in spring and summer (births peak in June). Life span probably 8–10 years, maximum 14

Related endangered species: Giant panda *(Ailuropoda melanoleuca)** EN

Status: IUCN EN; CITES I

While questions of classification puzzle zoologists, the lesser panda is facing serious problems of its own. Deforestation and competition for space and resources from ever-increasing human and livestock populations are threatening the animal throughout its range. Pandas are also frequently caught in traps intended for musk deer and sometimes find themselves the victims of armed conflicts in the areas they inhabit.

Lesser pandas *are nocturnal and arboreal, spending most of the day sleeping in the trees and feeding there by night.*

Pangolin, Long-Tailed

Manis tetradactyla

Asian species of pangolin have long been hunted for their scales, which are considered valuable in Chinese medicine. It is now feared that African long-tailed pangolins may suffer a similar threat.

Pangolins used to be classified alongside the anteaters and armadillos of South America because of anatomical similarities, lack of teeth, and a shared habit of catching ants and termites. Now, however, they are placed in an order by themselves. Their closest living relatives may in fact be carnivores such as otters and cats.

All pangolins have scaly plates covering the body, a soft, hairy belly, a long tongue, and no teeth. The scales are made of compressed hair and are slightly flexible, like our own fingernails.

The long-tailed pangolin—one of four African species—is a tree-dweller. At first sight its short legs may not seem particularly well adapted to climbing, but in the trees its long tail comes into its own. The tail is prehensile, which means that like those of harvest mice, chameleons, and some monkeys, it can be used to grip branches. A pangolin can even dangle upside down with its head pointing downward and the tail supporting its full body weight.

Forest Foragers

Pangolins move slowly when they are foraging, pausing often to examine crevices and loose bark for the telltale signs of insects beneath. Their long, curved claws provide excellent grip, but they also enable the animal to pry pieces of bark from living trees, thus exposing the nests of ants and termites. Often the animal will sit up on its haunches to reach a higher part of the nest. The insects are gathered up in large numbers on the animal's sticky tongue. The thick scales, armored head, and thick eyelids all help guard pangolins from ant and termite bites, and the nostrils and ears can also be closed to provide further protection.

DATA PANEL

Long-tailed pangolin (scaly anteater)

Manis tetradactyla

Family: Manidae

World population: Unknown

Distribution: Congo basin of western Central Africa, from Senegal in the northwest to Uganda

Habitat: Tropical rain forests

Size: Length head/body: 12–16 in (30–40 cm); tail: 23.5–27.5 in (60–70 cm). Weight: 4.4–6.6 lb (2–3 kg)

Form: Small animal with short legs, long claws, small, cone-shaped head, and long prehensile tail, tapering from thick base; upper body covered in large, brown overlapping scales; belly has dark hair; snout naked; eyes and ears small

Diet: Ants and other tree-dwelling insects

Breeding: One young born at any time of year; carried on mother's back or tail for first few months; mature at 2 years. Life span up to 20 years

Related endangered species: Temminck's ground pangolin (*Manis temminckii*) LRnt; Malayan pangolin (*M. javanicus*) LRnt; Indian pangolin (*M. crassicaudata*) LRnt; Chinese pangolin (*M. pentadactyla*) LRnt

Status: Not listed by IUCN; CITES II

See also: Luxury Products **1:** 46; Superstition **1:** 47; Armadillo, Giant **2:** 30

Pangolins *are extraordinary-looking creatures that have been likened to pinecones on legs because of their protective covering of overlapping horny scales.*

Although the pangolin's long claws make excellent tools, they are not much use as weapons of defense; given the chance, the animal would much rather flee than fight. The claws also get in the way if a pangolin is knocked to the ground, encumbering its movements so that it cannot run very fast. If a pangolin is cornered by an enemy, it curls into a tight ball, relying on its covering of scales for protection. Often it will jerk its body or snap the scales tight against its skin, trying to dig the sharp edges into the attacker. If a predator or a curious human attempts to uncurl a pangolin, it will make a sudden hissing sound, scrape its scales together, and squirt a foul-smelling liquid from a gland under its tail. These actions are enough to put off most attackers, but for a human hunter or collector it is easy work simply to scoop up the scaly ball and bundle it into a sack for transportation.

The Risk of Overexploitation

Live pangolins are sometimes taken for the zoo and pet trade, even though their adaptations for a forest life and diet of ants make them completely unsuited for life in captivity, and they usually die soon after capture. Despite this, their bizarre appearance means that many people seek them out as curios.

Many African tribes hunt pangolins mainly for their meat but also increasingly for their scales, which have long been prized as charms; they also play a role in rituals and in traditional medicine. In Africa such uses have always been on a small and possibly sustainable scale.

The situation is rather different, however, for the three Asian pangolin species, all of which have been overhunted for their meat, skin, and especially their scales, which are used in Chinese medicine. To supply this demand, tens of thousands of Asian pangolins have been killed. Concerns about the overexploitation of the Asian species have led to all three being listed in CITES Appendix II. Yet the listing may not have achieved the effect intended, for while it has effectively restricted the legal trade in pangolin parts, there are signs that it may simply have driven much of the commerce underground. Pangolin scales now fetch an even higher price than before on the black market, and conservationists are concerned that unscrupulous importers will soon seek to make money by exploiting African species, including the long-tailed pangolin, to supply the extra demand.

Panther, Florida

Puma concolor coryi

The last few individuals of the once-widespread Florida panther cling precariously to their remaining habitat in the southern United States. This handsome cat now faces possible extinction.

Like the ocelot, the panther (or puma) has a very wide distribution throughout North and South America. There are various local subspecies, one of which is the Florida panther. The panther has been extinct in Arkansas, Louisiana, Tennessee, and West Virginia since the 1950s. Another subspecies, the eastern panther, has probably also died out, leaving only the Florida panther in the eastern United States.

Almost everything that has happened to its environment in the last 100 years has hit the panther hard. It is a familiar story: As the human population has expanded and increased its activities, so panthers have been eliminated. They are large predators, presenting a threat to both people and their livestock. Farm animals have been attacked, and on average one person a year is killed by panthers in North America. These few attacks may not seem significant, but they give the animals a bad public image, cause widespread fear, and result in a desire to eliminate them. Consequently, in many states hunters have been employed to kill panthers.

However, the main cause of the panther losses in Florida is change to its habitat. The creation of new farmland areas from the dense bush and palmetto (small palm) thickets has deprived the panthers of living space. New highways slice through the remaining habitat, creating areas too small to support a viable population. Young panthers normally disperse between 18 and 50 miles (30 to 80 km) from where they were born, but then the fast-moving traffic on the roads poses a danger. Roads and other barriers prevent animals from mixing and meeting, and there is then more inbreeding and consequently a loss of genetic diversity. The species then faces the threat of breeding failure, including a higher proportion of birth defects and miscarriages.

Much of Florida lies on limestone overlaid by swamps. In recent times 40 percent of the swamplands have been lost as a result of expansion of farmland. Water is pumped from underground to

Alabama   Georgia
UNITED STATES

Florida

DATA PANEL

Florida panther

Puma concolor coryi

Family: Felidae

World population: Between 30 and 50

Distribution: South central Florida

Habitat: Swamp forest and dense thickets

Size: Length head/body: 42–54 in (100–130 cm); tail: 30–36 in (72–80 cm); height at shoulder: 26–31 in (62–75 cm). Weight: 66–125 lb (30–57 kg)

Form: Large, tawny or dark-brown cat with white flecks around the shoulders; long black-tipped tail, sharply kinked toward the end. Black on sides of face and backs of ears

Diet: Deer; also hares, rodents, armadillos; occasionally domestic animals

Breeding: One to 6 (usually 3) cubs born at almost any time of year after gestation period of about 3 months; mature at 2–3 years. Life span about 20 years

Related endangered species: Eastern panther (*Puma concolor cougar*) CR

Status: IUCN CR; CITES I

See also: Drainage and Irrigation **1:** 40; Inbreeding and Interbreeding **1:** 56, Jaguar **5:** 86; Ocelot, Texas **7:** 20

**The Florida
panther**

*population stands at
fewer than 50 today, but
the natural food supply
available in Florida would
once have supported about
1,300 panthers.*

supply towns and irrigate crops. Swamps
therefore dry up, and whole areas of forest and
scrub become more susceptible to fire. Fire is
devastating, not only because it kills wildlife, but also
because it removes vital cover from large areas. The
deer that form the main prey of the panthers are
deprived of their food by the fires and also by the
replacement of native vegetation by introduced plants
(such as Brazilian pepper) that they do not eat, and
the losses of deer affect the panther population.

In addition, panthers are at the end of a long food
chain and therefore susceptible to the toxic materials
that accumulate in their prey. Burning of domestic and
industrial refuse in Florida gives out pollutants, which
collect at every level of the food chain.

Chances of Survival

Legally protected since 1973, the Florida panther now
survives only in and around the Everglades National
Park and Big Cypress National Preserve. In 1995 eight
females of the Texas subspecies were imported to
provide fresh genes, and in 1980 a sperm bank was
started to enable continued breeding of the animals.
Major roads have now been fenced to reduce
accidents with traffic, and habitat "corridors" are
being created to allow safer movement. Nevertheless,
the panther's future in Florida still looks bleak.

Paradisefish, Ornate

Malpulutta kretseri

The ornate paradisefish is found in streams deep in the jungle of southwestern Sri Lanka. It is a tiny, bubble-blowing jewel of a fish whose numbers are low in the wild. Since 1998 it has been protected in a unique agreement between the island authorities and ornamental aquatic industry.

The IUCN lists the ornate paradisefish as Lower Risk, conservation dependent. In this situation remedial action is usually taken to save a species from becoming Vulnerable or Endangered. In the case of the ornate paradisefish, however, it is not known why numbers are low in the wild. Indeed, it is possible that its scarcity does not indicate a declining population at all; instead, it may represent longstanding stability. Evidence seems to suggest that the fish is perhaps even more abundant today than it was in the past. Nonetheless, in Sri Lanka the species is regarded as Uncommon, Threatened, or Endangered.

Pollution can largely be discounted as a reason for the low population size since the fish inhabits remote forest streams, far away from human activities. Overcollection can also be ruled out, since there is not a great demand for ornate paradisefish by aquarists, despite its undoubted beauty. Specialized hobbyists who concentrate on anabantoids (labyrinth fish) have in the past bought small numbers of wild-caught ornate paradisefish. However, today's (still limited) supply comes from the aquarium-bred offspring of these original specimens. The fish are often exchanged between members of anabantoid-keeping and breeding associations or sold to local specialized aquatic outlets.

Some authorities believe that the two known forms of ornate paradisefish—distinguishable by their color—in fact represent separate subspecies: *Malpulutta kretseri kretseri* (inhabiting the Bentota Basin) and *Malpulutta kretseri minor* (a form with blue fin edges, found in the Kalu Basin). There is also a violet-colored variant.

Bubble-Nest Breeding

The paradisefish has fascinating breeding behavior. As in many other labyrinth fish (freshwater spiny-finned fish with a special respiratory organ), the male builds a

---

DATA PANEL

Ornate paradisefish

Malpulutta kretseri

Family: Belontiidae

World population: Unknown

Distribution: Southwestern Sri Lanka: Colombo-Galle-Ratnapura triangle

Habitat: Small, shady, shallow streams—often silted and containing abundant submerged leaf debris—in forested areas

Size: Up to 2.4 in (6 cm) reported, but wild-caught specimens average only 0.8 in (2 cm)

Form: Tiny labyrinth fish; brilliantly colored scales. Male's coloration intensifies during mating displays. Breathes air with use of auxiliary respiratory organ

Diet: Small aquatic invertebrates

Breeding: Male builds bubble-nest and attracts female to it; spawning embraces occur, and up to 200 eggs are laid. Male guards eggs until they hatch (2 days). Hatchlings are free-swimming after 3–5 days

Related endangered species: Combtail (*Belontia signata*) LRcd

Status: IUCN LRcd; not listed by CITES

See also: Organizations 1: 10; Captive Breeding 1: 87; Archerfish, Western 2: 28; Lungfish, Australian 6: 50; Rocky, Eastern Province 8: 40

The ornate paradisefish is a tiny, colorful, air-breathing fish that is only found in the shady jungle streams of southwestern Sri Lanka, where it is protected.

nest of mucus-covered bubbles under a submerged leaf or, occasionally, in a sheltered spot on the surface of a shallow pool. Following a long series of impressive displays during which the male extends his fins and intensifies his brilliant coloration, the pair repeatedly embrace under the bubbles. When the female releases each small batch of eggs, they are immediately fertilized by the male. The pair (but more often the female) then gather the sinking eggs in their mouths and blow them into the bubble-nest. The procedure is repeated until between 100 and 200 eggs are laid over a period of time, which can be as short as one hour or as long as 12 hours. Once all the eggs are laid, the female leaves, and the male stands guard until the eggs hatch about two days later. The fry (young fish) become free-swimming some three to five days after hatching.

Securing a Future

In 1998 continuing concern about the relatively low abundance of the species in the wild led to a resolution: Sri Lanka's ornamental fish exporters and the island's authorities agreed to ban exportation of all wild-caught specimens. Instead, permission was granted for small numbers of paradisefish to be collected from several localities and for captive-breeding programs to be established using the specimens as breeding stock.

In order to get the program successfully underway, and to avoid some of the major difficulties of breeding such a challenging species, the Anabantoid Association of Great Britain contributed data that had been collected from members with direct experience in spawning paradisefish in aquariums. Within a few months the first success was reported. Others followed soon after, indicating that the future of this tiny labyrinth fish may now be reasonably secure.

Parrot, Night

Geopsittacus occidentalis

A relative of the budgerigar, the night parrot of the Australian outback is one of the world's least known and most rarely seen birds. It is assumed to have a tiny population, and its range is unknown. Although sightings have become rarer, it may not be currently declining.

The unusual night parrot has always been shrouded in mystery. Although it was described by observers as common in parts of South Australia during the 1870s and 1880s, it seems even then to have been extremely elusive. Since that time there have been only a handful of authenticated records, with most sightings remaining unconfirmed. In fact, until very recently the species was thought to be possibly extinct.

Despite two publicity campaigns and at least five dedicated searches for night parrots, there has been only one authenticated sighting over the last 15 years.

A night parrot was reported on October 17, 1990, in the Mount Isa Uplands, 22 miles (36 km) south of the settlement of Boulia in northwestern Queensland.

Nocturnal Habits

One of the problems facing those searching for the night parrot is suggested by its common name, since, unusually for a parrot, it is nocturnal in its habits. (The only other habitually nocturnal parrot is the kakapo of New Zealand—see **5:** 90.) Historical accounts refer to the bird roosting during the day among shrubs, under dense clumps of spinifex grass, even in caves or in tunnels that it dug into the sandy desert soil. The birds were reported to leave their roosts late in the evening, either singly, in pairs, or in small groups, in order to visit the nearest water source before feeding. They would then usually return to water several more times in the course of the night.

The parrot's dark, barred plumage has always made it hard to spot—a problem compounded by the bird's reaction when disturbed. Instead of taking flight, it prefers to run. Even when pursued closely, it flies for only a short distance a few feet off the ground before diving into dense vegetation and running off at right angles to its line of flight to be quickly lost from view.

Because of the difficulty of getting more than a glimpse of the furtive bird, some claimed reports may in fact be mistaken sightings of other parrots. The ground parrot, its closest relative, is superficially similar in appearance, although it has a longer tail and a different

---

DATA PANEL

Night parrot

Geopsittacus occidentalis

Family: Psittacidae

World population: Unknown; perhaps fewer than 50 birds

Distribution: Australian outback

Habitat: Arid and semiarid plains; spinifex grassland or goosefoot and samphire shrublands on floodplains, claypans, or by watercourses or salt lakes; recently in rolling plains of Mitchell grass with scattered goosefoot shrubs

Size: Length: 8.5–10 in (22–25 cm); wingspan: 17–18 in (44–46 cm)

Form: Smallish parrot with stocky build and short tail. Bright yellowish-green below breast with dark mottling and barring except on belly; upper wing has dark-grayish flight feathers and

pale-yellow wingbar; underwing grayish-green with broader yellow wingbar; tail browner

Diet: Reported to feed on seeds of grasses and other plants

Breeding: Virtually unknown; nests described as being of small sticks or leaves in clump of vegetation at end of tunnel or runway made in soil; clutch may be 2–4 eggs, possibly up to 6

Related endangered species: Eleven in the subfamily Platycercinae to which the night parrot belongs, including golden-shouldered parrot (*Psephotus chrysopterygius*) EN; swift parrot (*Lathamus discolor*) EN; and orange-bellied parrot (*Neophema chrysogaster*) CR

Status: IUCN CR; CITES I and II

Range and population size uncertain
AUSTRALIA

See also: Introductions **1:** 54; Kakapo **5:** 90; Kea **5:** 92

range and habitat. In contrast, another relative, the budgerigar, could hardly be more different, being abundant in many parts of Australia and also known around the world as a cage bird. The budgerigar is distinctly smaller, however, and active by day.

There have been unconfirmed reports of night parrot sightings from all the mainland states of Australia and from the Northern Territory, so it is possible that the bird survives at low densities over much of its former range in the arid and semiarid regions of the outback. This vast area covers more than 1 million square miles (2.6 million sq. km), helping to explain why the bird is so hard to find.

Although there is too little information available at present to allow for any clear estimate of the parrot's numbers, the scarcity of recorded sightings over the past 120 years almost certainly reflects a real decline in its abundance. Locating a viable population is vital if the night parrot is to be rescued from its plight.

Likely Threats

In the absence of hard evidence, the threats thought most likely to endanger the ground-nesting night parrot include predation by nonnative mammals, especially wild cats and foxes. An early report of the parrot's disappearance from Innaminka Station, South Australia, in the 1880s coincided with the introduction of large numbers of cats from New South Wales. Another account referred to many night parrots being killed by cats near

Alice Springs, Northern Territory, in 1892. The birds may also suffer competition for food from cattle and other livestock. Rabbits are another source of competition for night parrots, eating their food and damaging their habitat. In addition, the birds' water supplies may have been reduced by the spread of wild camels, descendants of animals that were introduced to arid areas between the 1880s and early 1900s for transporting people and goods.

There is an urgent need to find the remaining birds, perhaps through the use of trained dog teams; the species could then be helped by captive-breeding programs, using techniques developed for ground parrots. Once a site is found to contain night parrots, other targets will include researching the birds' ecology, controlling threats from predators, and reversing the damage caused by habitat degradation.

The night parrot *is unusual not just in its nocturnal habits that have given it its name, but also for its ground-nesting behavior.*

Peafowl, Congo

Afropavo congensis

Lacking the spectacular train of the two Asian peafowls—the blue, or Indian peafowl and the green, or Javanese peafowl—the smaller Congo peafowl has a more subtle beauty. Unknown to science until 65 years ago, it now faces threats from hunting and loss of habitat.

The discovery of the Congo peafowl during the 1930s was one of the major ornithological events of the 20th century. Not only was it remarkable that such a large, brightly plumaged bird could have remained undiscovered by ornithologists in an area that had already been relatively well explored, but also because up until then pheasants—of which peafowls are a subgroup—were not thought to occur naturally anywhere outside Asia and the extreme eastern fringes of Europe.

The discovery itself is a remarkable story. In 1913 an American ornithologist, James Chapin, was staying in the Ituri Forest area of the then Belgian Congo when he spotted a bird feather in a tribal chief's headdress that he was unable to identify as belonging to any known Congo bird.

Twenty-one years later, in another coincidence, he was visiting a museum in the Congo when he noticed two stuffed birds in a dark hallway that he did not recognize. Although they were labeled as imported young Indian peacocks, they were clearly not of that species. His suspicions aroused, Chapin wrote to have the strange headdress feather sent to him. When he received it, he found that it exactly matched the wing feathers of one of the mystery birds. In this roundabout way Chapin discovered a bird new to science, and in 1936 he returned to the Ituri forest and collected seven Congo peafowls.

Little-Known Bird

Shy and retiring, the beautiful Congo peafowl spends much of its time hiding in dense undergrowth. Hard to find, it has remained little known since its discovery; although local people knew where it was, it was rarely recorded by ornithologists until recently.

Field research carried out between 1993 and 1995 found the Congo peafowl to be present in 13 out of 20 survey areas. It also revealed new sites for the species that extended its

DATA PANEL

Congo peafowl (Congo peacock)

Afropavo congensis

Family: Phasianidae

World population: Estimated at 2,500–10,000 birds

Distribution: Central and eastern Democratic Republic of Congo

Habitat: Lowland and foothill forest

Size: Length: 25–27.5 in (64–70 cm); female slightly smaller than male

Form: Large gamebird with relatively small head. Male has dense white tuft of bristly feathers in front of shorter black crest of downy feathers on black crown. Naked blue skin around eyes, naked red throat. Glossy dark bronzy-green upperparts, black underparts with greenish gloss, and violet-blue gloss on breast, wing, and end of tail feathers. Female has shorter brown crown tuft on brownish-red head, brownish-white chin, glossy green

upperparts with brownish-gold eyelike markings, brown-barred and mottled reddish-brown breast and flanks; rest of underparts black. Legs grayish, with pair of prominent spurs in males

Diet: Seeds and fruit of trees and other plants of forest understory; also termites and larvae, ants, aquatic insects, and other invertebrates

Breeding: Monogamous (1 mate); breeding season may depend on rainfall; 2–4 reddish-brown to cream eggs laid in hollow or flat area 5–10 ft (1.5–3 m) in tree branches; incubated by female for 3.5–4 weeks; young cared for by both parents, fledging in only 6 days

Related endangered species: Green peafowl (*Pavo muticus*) VU; 22 other pheasant species are threatened

Status: IUCN VU; not listed by CITES

CENTRAL AFRICAN
REPUBLIC
SUDAN
UGANDA
REPUBLIC
OF CONGO
DEMOCRATIC
REPUBLIC
OF CONGO
RWANDA
BURUNDI
TANZANIA
ANGOLA
ZAMBIA

See also: Research **1:** 84; National Parks **1:** 92; Guan, Horned **5:** 44; Malleefowl **6:** 64; Tragopan, Temminck's **9:** 94
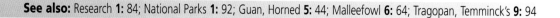

range northeast. During more recent searches the bird was found in other areas where it had not been recorded before, and it may yet prove to have a still wider range. Despite such new finds, the surveys indicate that there are large areas within its expected range where it does not seem to occur, suggesting that the total population is isolated in small, fragmented subpopulations.

Multiple Threats

Although it was held in high regard by tribal culture, the Congo peafowl is known to have been hunted for food by local people, and hunting continues. It is probably also widely captured in snares set for antelopes and small mammals.

Mining operations, subsistence agriculture, and logging destroy or degrade the bird's habitat. In addition, mining and the associated human settlement it brings result in remote areas of forest becoming opened up to exploitation, leading in turn to an increase in hunting—both on a subsistence level and for sale in local markets. The huge numbers of Rwandan refugees who have settled in the eastern Democratic Republic of Congo since 1994 are likely to add considerably to the pressures from hunting and loss of habitat.

One way of reducing any further decline is by effective conservation of the subpopulations that live in protected areas such as Maiko National Park, one of the species' strongholds, and there is a strong possibility that hunting can be banned or at least limited.

The Congo peafowl
was unknown to science until 1936, following a search that began in 1913 with a single unidentified feather from a tribal headdress.

Pelican, Dalmatian

Pelecanus crispus

The largest of the world's seven species of pelicans, the Dalmatian pelican suffered massive population declines during the 19th and 20th centuries. A series of conservation initiatives have resulted in stable or increasing populations over much of its range.

Among the largest and heaviest of all flying birds, Dalmatian pelicans are good swimmers and graceful, efficient fliers. A pelican uses its huge pouched beak as a kind of net for catching fish. It swims along with its neck erect. Having spotted a suitable prey, it makes a sudden lunge and opens its bill underwater to trap the fish—together with as many as 3.6 gallons (13.6 liters) of water—in its cavernous pouch. The pelican then takes its head and neck out of the water, allows some water to drain off, and swallows its catch.

Dalmatian pelicans live and breed in a variety of wetlands, mainly inland by slow-flowing rivers, lakes, and marshes, but also by coastal lagoons, deltas, and estuaries. While they prefer to fish close to their breeding or roosting areas, they can travel great distances over land. They forage singly or in groups of between two and five birds that often cooperate with each other. Swimming in a horseshoe pattern, the birds open their wings every 20 seconds or so to drive fish into the shallows where they are more easily caught. Each bird needs 2.3 to 2.6 pounds (1 to 1.2 kg) of fish per day. Dalmatian pelicans rarely eat anything other than fish and seem incapable of adjusting to feed on other prey, so colonies usually abandon waters from which fish have disappeared.

A History of Disturbance

Dalmatian pelicans have suffered much at the hands of people over the centuries. They once had a wider range, breeding as far north as southern Britain in Neolithic times and on large estuaries such as the Rhine and Elbe Rivers in northwestern Europe

---

DATA PANEL

Dalmatian pelican

Pelecanus crispus

Family: Pelecanidae

World population: 15,000–20,000 birds, including 4,000–5,000 breeding pairs

Distribution: Breeds in parts of eastern Europe and eastern Central Asia. European breeders winter in eastern Mediterranean; Russian and Central Asian breeders winter in Middle East and Indian subcontinent; Mongolian breeders winter in eastern China

Habitat: Mainly freshwater wetlands inland; also river deltas and coastal lagoons

Size: Length (with neck extended): 5.25–6 ft (1.6–1.8 m), including beak up to 18 in (45 cm); wingspan: 10–11.5 ft (3.1–3.5 m). Weight: 22–26 lb (10–12 kg)

Form: Huge waterbird; oversized bill has an elastic skin pouch for scooping up fish; long neck usually retracted in a curve; plumage white with a gray tinge; yellow breast patch; curly feathers on nape of neck. Eyes with pale iris surrounded by small area of pale skin. Throat sac becomes red when breeding; gray underwings show central white band and have dark feathers only at tips. Juveniles are pale gray-brown above, whitish below

Diet: Fish, especially carp, perch, rudd, pike, and eel

Breeding: Breeds in colonies in late March–early July; builds large, untidy nest of grass, water plants, reeds, and twigs, cemented by droppings. Female usually lays 2–3 white eggs, incubated by both sexes for 4 weeks. Young leave nest at 1 month and gather in groups called pods; fledging period about 12 weeks; mature at 3–4 years

Related endangered species: Spot-billed pelican *(Pelecanus philippensis)* VU

Status: IUCN LRcd; CITES I

See also: Drainage and Irrigation **1:** 40; Bustard, Great **3:** 10; Cormorant, Galápagos **3:** 64

until Roman times. During the 19th century millions lived in Romania alone. Today the entire world breeding population is estimated to be between 4,000 and 5,000 pairs.

The main causes of the dramatic decline has been the massive drainage of wetlands for agriculture and other development and also direct persecution. It has become increasingly difficult for the birds to find undisturbed sites for breeding, and fish stocks have dwindled in some waters as a result of overfishing.

Wetlands are still being reclaimed or adversely altered by damming, overfishing, or other developments, as well as pollution from pesticides and other sources. Tourism and the fishing industry cause disturbance to breeding colonies and may reduce breeding success or cause the birds to abandon nests altogether. A recent and serious problem is that the pelicans are prone to flying into power cables.

The population is still declining in Mongolia, where a different threat exists. Here herders kill the pelicans for the upper mandibles (jaws) of their bills, traditionally used for horse-grooming tools.

Reducing the Threats

In recent years overall numbers seem to have stabilized as conservation programs have reduced the impact of the major threats in Europe. They include providing artificial breeding platforms, marking or removing power lines, employing wardens to protect key sites, and educating fishing communities about the pelicans. It is also proposed to improve legal protection for the birds and their habitat, monitor numbers and ecological changes at key sites, and develop public awareness. Without such action the Dalmatian pelican could be back on the threatened list within five years.

Dalmatian pelicans are among the largest of living birds. Their enormous bills can be up to 18 inches (45 cm) long.

Penguin, Galápagos

Spheniscus mendiculus

The only species of penguin to live on the Equator, the portly Galápagos penguin breeds on at least five of the Galápagos Islands. Because of its restricted range and very small population, a sharp decline in numbers is particularly disturbing.

Penguins are normally associated with cold habitats in and around Antarctica, although several species have ranges that include warmer climates. The Humboldt penguin, for instance, breeds in coastal Chile and Peru. However, the Galápagos penguin—a close relative of the Humboldt—is the only species that lives entirely within the tropics, on at least five islands of the Galápagos group. Life at such latitudes is challenging for the birds, since their insulating plumage, underlying fat, and specialized blood heat exchange—all adaptations for surviving in very cold water—make it difficult for them to cope with the tropical heat when on land. Temperatures in the Galápagos Islands can rise to more than 104°F (40°C).

Adaptations to Heat

In order to survive the heat, the Galápagos penguin has various anatomical and behavioral adaptations. It is one of the smallest penguin species, and the smaller an animal, the greater its surface area relative to its total size. Consequently, the Galápagos penguin has a large surface area from which to dissipate (lose) heat when on land. Heat loss is made easier by its having shorter feathers than any other species of penguin.

When ashore, the adults seek shade. They lose more heat by increasing the blood flow to their flippers, feet, and bare facial patches. The flippers are proportionately larger than those of cold-climate penguins, increasing the area where heat exchange can take place. The animals' blood supply can also bypass the heat-transfer system that helps maintain their body temperature in cold water. Galápagos penguins often breed in rock crevices and caves, such as lava tubes (natural tunnels in lava flows) that shade the birds and their chicks from the sun.

Major Threats

The Galápagos penguin depends directly on the surrounding ocean for its survival.

DATA PANEL

Galápagos penguin

Spheniscus mendiculus

Family: Spheniscidae

World population: Fluctuates greatly; currently estimated at 1,200 individuals

Distribution: Galápagos Islands, Ecuador

Habitat: Breeds on low-lying areas of coastal, volcanic desert, rarely more than 55 yards (50 m) inland; feeds around upwellings of cool, nutrient-rich inshore waters

Size: Length: 19–21 in (48–53 cm); height: 14 in (35 cm). Weight: average 3.8–5.7 lb (1.7–2.6 kg)

Form: Small with black head; white stripes on face; black to brownish back and tail; chin and underparts white; variable pattern of black spots and irregular black bands on breast; flippers brown-black above, white below; male more boldly marked. Juveniles have grayish upperparts and lack distinctive face pattern

Diet: Schools of ocean fish, including sardines and mullet. Possibly crustaceans

Breeding: Breeds at any time, in small colonies or singly, when food supply is adequate; nests in lava tubes, rock crevices, or caves, at least partly shaded from the sun; 2 white eggs laid per breeding attempt; pair shares incubation that lasts 5–6 weeks; young leave nest at 8.5–9 weeks

Related endangered species: Nine other penguin species are threatened, including African penguin (*Spheniscus demersus*) VU; Humboldt penguin (*S. humboldti*) VU; erect-crested penguin (*Eudyptes sclateri*) EN; Snares penguin (*E. robustus*) VU

Status: IUCN EN; not listed by CITES

COSTA RICA

PANAMA

COLOMBIA

Galápagos Islands (Ecuador)

ECUADOR

PERU

See also: Biomes 1: 18; Introductions 1: 54; Gull, Lava 5: 46; Iguana, Galápagos Marine (see text on El Niño) 5: 78

The Cromwell Current, an upwelling of cool, nutrient-rich water, maintains the fish stocks that the penguins rely on for food. The current is susceptible to a periodic climatic event called the El Niño Southern Oscillation (ENSO). Records show that a population of 3,400 penguins declined by 77 percent between 1982 and 1983—an ENSO year that adversely affected the Cromwell Current, reducing fish stocks and causing thousands of birds to starve. It is likely that more females than males died, which would have slowed the recovery of the population. Another ENSO event in 1997 caused a further decline of 66 percent.

Galápagos penguins are known to be slow breeders, the birth rate averaging out at only 1.3 chicks per year. In ENSO years the entire population can fail to breed at all. The animals also have a restricted breeding range, with about 95 percent nesting on just two islands. Chicks and eggs are vulnerable to natural predators such as rice rats, snakes, and crabs. More serious threats are posed by introduced predators, including feral dogs, cats, and brown and black rats, which kill adults and chicks.

Galápagos penguins
feed on the rich fish stocks around the Galápagos Islands. The small, dapper bird has large flippers and feet that help it dissipate body heat.

A tenfold increase in the permanent human population of the Galápagos in the last 40 years has led to disturbance of breeding sites and an expansion of coastal fisheries. Penguins are caught in nets and suffer from competition for fish stocks. Tourism adds to disruption; visitors come to look at the birds.

To ensure the continued survival of the Galápagos penguin, controls on fisheries, oil spills, human disturbance, and the introduction of mammalian predators are urgently required, as are scientific studies of the penguins to help increase their breeding success rate. Most importantly, we need to cut fossil fuel emissions to reduce global warming, which is likely to increase ENSO events.

Petrel, Bermuda

Pterodroma cahow

The story of this graceful seabird is an extraordinary saga of rediscovery after hundreds of years of presumed extinction, followed by a steady increase in numbers due to the efforts of conservationists. The population is still dangerously small, however, and the bird continues to face several threats.

Bermuda is made up of about 150 small islands in the northwestern Atlantic Ocean, 750 miles (1,200 km) off the east coast of the United States. As well as serving as a useful stopover site in spring and fall for windblown migrants, it is home to one of the world's rarest seabirds, the Bermuda petrel.

Also known as the cahow in imitation of its eerie mating calls, the bird is one of the so-called gadfly petrels of the *Pterodroma* genus. They are graceful, long-winged birds, fast in flight, alternating bursts of rapid wingbeats with long glides. They rarely alight on the water, feeding on the wing by seizing small sea creatures such as squid from just below the water's surface with their sharp, hooked bills. In contrast, they are awkward on land, managing only a shuffling walk due to the position of their feet at the back of their bodies. To avoid the attentions of predators, the birds visit their colonies only under cover of darkness.

Lost and Found

Bermuda remained uninhabited until 1609, when an English expedition was shipwrecked there. At the time the islands teemed with seabirds, including vast numbers of Bermuda petrels. Soon, however, settlers arrived in force, bringing with them pigs, rats, and other animals that raided the petrels' nesting burrows. To make matters worse, the settlers themselves also caught and ate huge numbers of the birds, until by 1621 the species was thought to be extinct.

No specimens were recorded for more than 300 years, but then, miraculously, the bird turned up again. The first clue that it still existed came in 1906, when a dead petrel was found on Castle Island, one of the smallest in Bermuda. At first it was taken to be a previously unknown capped petrel from the

DATA PANEL

Bermuda petrel (cahow)

Pterodroma cahow

Family: Procellariidae

World population: About 180 birds

Distribution: Breeds on a few islets in Castle Harbor, Bermuda; outside the breeding season (mid-June–October) the birds live at sea, probably wandering across the Atlantic Ocean; has been recorded off North Carolina

Habitat: Breeds on rocky islets; spends nonbreeding season flying over open ocean

Size: Length: 15 in (38 cm); wingspan: 35 in (89 cm)

Form: Medium-sized, long-winged, short-tailed seabird with hooked black bill bearing nostrils in tubes on top; webbed feet set at hind end of body

Diet: Little known; probably mainly squid and crustaceans, plus some fish

Breeding: January to mid-June; colonies once nested in burrows in soil, but now use natural crevices in soft limestone and artificial burrows; single, large white egg is incubated for 7–8 weeks; young fledge in 13–14 weeks

Related endangered species: Thirty-five other petrel and shearwater species are threatened, and a further 2 are extinct. In the *Pterodroma* genus to which the Bermuda petrel belongs they include: Chatham Islands petrel (*Pterodroma axillaris*) CR; Galápagos petrel (*P. phaeopygia*) CR; Jamaica petrel (*P. caribbaea*) CR; black-capped petrel (*P. hasitata*) EN; Barau's petrel (*P. baraui*) EN; Trindade petrel (*P. arminjoniana*) VU; Atlantic petrel (*P. incerta*) VU; Murphy's petrel (*P. ultima*) LRnt

Status: IUCN EN; not listed by CITES

See also: Pesticides **1**: 51; Climate Change **1**: 53; Heat, Noise, and Light **1**: 52; Albatross, Wandering **2**: 8

Caribbean region, but then in 1916 another individual turned up—and it seemed to fit 17th-century descriptions of the missing species. The clinching record came in 1931, when a bird that hit St. David's lighthouse was retrieved and identified as a Bermuda petrel. Another definite record was of an individual that struck a telephone pole in St. George, at the northeastern end of the main island.

The puzzle of where these birds came from remained, since none could be found nesting on any of the inhabited islands. In 1951 a search turned up 18 pairs of the petrels nesting on rocky islets in Castle Harbor, near St. George. The total area of these islets was only 2.4 acres (1 ha). Instead of nesting in burrows as they had done in the 17th century, the petrels were now using natural crevices created by water erosion of the soft limestone rock, since there was little soil on the islets.

The Bermuda petrel was considered extinct for more than 300 years and was only rediscovered in the early years of the 20th century.

Building Up the Numbers

After its rediscovery the tiny breeding population was carefully observed. Worryingly, numbers increased only slightly in the early years; by 1961 there were still only 20 pairs. Like all other members of the tubenose order, which includes albatrosses and shearwaters as well as petrels, Bermuda petrels are slow breeders: Roosting birds lay a single egg, and the young take five or more years to become sexually mature.

Subsequently, research into the reasons for the petrels' poor productivity revealed that one problem facing the birds came in the shape of another seabird, the white-tailed tropicbird, which competed for the rock crevices where the petrels bred, killing the young in the nest after they hatched. Conservationists built artificial burrows for the petrels, but these too were attacked. Eventually, researchers solved the problem by fitting stone or wooden baffles over the burrow entrances that allowed the petrels to pass in but kept the bulkier tropicbirds out. This has had some success: The population is increasing, and breeding success is up to 25 percent from 5 percent in the 1950s.

A lingering threat comes from DDT and other pollutants, which become concentrated in the petrels' bodies and may be responsible for the growing number of eggs that fail to hatch. The bright lights of a nearby airport and NASA tracking station also cause problems by disrupting the petrels' nighttime aerial courtship rituals. More worrying still is the risk of rising sea levels as a result of global warming; after 25 years without major problems half a dozen serious floods affected petrel burrows in the 1990s. Conservationists have replanted other potential breeding islands with native flora; at some future time a new colony may be established on one of them, Nonsuch Island.

Pig, Visayan Warty

Sus cebifrons

The Visayan warty pig has only recently been recognized as a distinct species, but its decline has been so dramatic that many conservationists fear it may suffer the fate of becoming extinct before any detailed studies of its biology can be made.

The Visayan warty pig is named after an island group, the Visayas, in the central Philippines. In 1987, when the species was first described, the Visayan warty pig was thought to be widespread in the Philippines, with populations on the islands of Negros, Panay, Leyte, Samar, Billiran, and Bohol. Only six years later it seemed that all but the Panay and Negros populations had already disappeared. Genetic changes spread faster through small, isolated populations, so islands often have more than their fair share of unique types of animal. These so-called "endemic" species are always vulnerable to extinction because they have nowhere to move to if their habitat changes. That is just what has happened to the Visayan warty pig. The species is a close relative of other Southeast Asian wild pigs, but in the isolation of the Philippine Islands it evolved into something different.

Deforestation

The human population of the Philippines has increased rapidly, and consequently the pigs' natural habitat of dense tropical rain forest has been almost completely destroyed. Some of the forests have been lost to loggers and large-scale farmers, but local people, who clear small areas at a time and farm them for a few years, are also destroying significant areas.

When the rainy season comes, the soil is quickly washed away from such plots, and they become useless. Soil washed off the land ends up being dumped at sea by rivers and streams, where it destroys coral reefs and fish nursery grounds. The ecological disaster that is developing in the Philippines is not helped by prolonged periods of political and economic hardship, which means that conservation issues are not given attention.

A few organizations are now trying to help the Philippine government by taking responsibility for reef and forest conservation, but it may already be to late for the islands' most recently discovered mammal.

DATA PANEL

Visayan warty pig

Sus cebifrons

Family: Suidae

World population: Unknown

Distribution: Two Philippine islands: Panay and Negros

Habitat: Rain forest; ventures onto cleared land to feed

Size: Length head/body: 35–40 in (90–102 cm); tail: 12–15 in (30–40 cm); height to shoulder: 22–35 in (50–90 cm). Weight: 100–220 lb (45–100 kg)

Form: Small, dark wild pig; stout, hair-covered bodies and short legs

Diet: Almost anything edible that can be found on the ground or in soft soil

Breeding: Unknown, but probably similar to other species of wild pig. Life span 25 years or more

Related endangered species: Babirusa (*Babyrousa babyrussa*)* VU; many other wild pigs

Status: IUCN CR; not listed by CITES

Luzon

PHILIPPINES

Samar

Palawan

Panay

Negros

Mindanao

MALAYSIA
BRUNEI

Borneo

See also: Island Biogeography **1:** 30; Inbreeding and Interbreeding **1:** 56; Babirusa **2:** 44

Competition for Food

Lack of official protection is not the Visayan warty pig's only problem. With an ever-increasing human population to feed and farmland in such short supply it is difficult for local people to see an animal that eats their crops as anything other than a pest. However, in a vicious circle of events the more forest that is cleared for agriculture, the less natural food is available for the wild pigs. The pigs probably used to survive quite happily by rummaging around on the forest floor for roots, shoots, fungi, fallen fruits, and nuts. Now that the forest has gone, however, a pig's only chance to eke out an existence is often to venture out from fragments of cover to raid fields of crops.

All species of pigs are attractive to hungry people and offer a fine supply of good free meat. Pigs are therefore commonly hunted and snared. Wild pigs

The Visayan warty pig remained officially unknown to science as a separate species until 1987. Part of the reason it came to light then was the rapid destruction of its forest habitat, which made it easier to obtain specimens. It is usually found in groups of four or five individuals.

often interbreed with domestic ones, creating hybrids and resulting in the genetic extinction of purebred species in the wild.

A combination of these threats has already caused major reductions in populations of other wild pigs in Eastern Asia. For example, the Javan pig is on the brink of extinction, and the Vietnamese warty pig of Laos may also have gone by now. Other wild pigs of Palawan, Malaysia, and the Ryukyu Islands (Japan) have been severely endangered too and are now classified by the IUCN as Vulnerable.

69

Pigeon, Pink

Columba mayeri

Thanks to the dedicated work of conservationists, the pink pigeon has been saved from extinction, and numbers have dramatically increased over the last decade. But without continued intensive management, including a captive-breeding program, the species would be likely to become extinct.

A close relative of the abundant and widespread wood pigeon of Europe and parts of Asia, the pink pigeon is one of the most attractive members of the large family of pigeons and doves. This group has suffered more than most from extinction, with almost a third of the 309 surviving species classified as Threatened or Lower Risk, near threatened. Over 80 percent of them are island species, as were all but one of the 13 species of pigeons and doves that have recently become extinct.

The pink pigeon is found only on the island of Mauritius and the neighboring Ile aux Aigrettes. Discoveries of bones of the birds indicate that it was once widespread in forests throughout the whole of Mauritius. Now it is confined to the southwestern part of the island. The precarious position the species is in today is entirely due to a variety of human factors.

Multiple Threats

Along with many other unique animals and plants, the pink pigeon has suffered from the massive destruction of the native forests of Mauritius by colonists from the late 18th century onward. Uncontrolled hunting also played its part in reducing the species to a perilously low and fragmented population.

In addition, the pink pigeon—and other unique Mauritian wildlife—has been affected by predation by the legion of animals deliberately introduced or accidentally brought to the island by sailors and settlers. They include the crab-eating macaque, originally from Southeast Asia, which preys on adult pigeons, also taking eggs and young from their nests. The small Indian mongoose, which was introduced to control black rats, also preys on young pigeons. However, black rats that take the pigeon's eggs and young have survived and prospered; feral cats are also predators of pigeons.

Other threats affecting the birds include disease and shortages of suitable food in late winter. The remaining small and fragmented populations and their forest habitat are increasingly at the mercy of tropical cyclones that hit the island from time to time. Winds blowing at up to 155 miles per hour (250 km/h) or more not only damage the forest by stripping trees of the shoots and fruit on which the pigeons feed but also blow down the bird's nests.

By 1990, as a result of all these factors, the total world population of this once common species was reduced to just 10 individuals, all of which nested in a single grove of introduced Japanese red cedar trees.

Rescue Plans

The pink pigeon has been the focus of a major international rescue program for many years. It has involved sponsorship by BirdLife International (a global partnership of conservation organizations), the World Wide Fund for Nature, and the New York Zoological Society. There is also a long-term program of research and rescue involving the Mauritian government working together with several zoos—the Durrell Wildlife Conservation Trust, Vogelpark Walsrode in Germany, and the New York and Alberquerque zoos.

Attempts at captive breeding at the zoos began in the mid-1970s. Careful reintroduction into the wild has recently helped achieve a dramatic increase in the pigeon's numbers. Other elements in the program

70

See also: Organizations **1:** 10; Introductions **1:** 54; Natural Disasters **1:** 57; Pigeon, Victoria Crowned **7:** 72

DATA PANEL

Pink pigeon (Mauritius pink pigeon, chestnut-tailed pigeon)

Columba mayeri

Family: Columbidae

World population: 360–380 birds

Distribution: Restricted to 4 sites in southwestern Mauritius and introduced to Ile aux Aigrettes, off eastern coast

Habitat: Subtropical evergreen forests, including remnant native trees and introduced species; most pairs nest in introduced Japanese red cedars

Size: Length:14–14.8 in (36–40 cm). Weight: male 8.5–14.5 oz (240–410 g); female 7.5–13 oz (213–369 g)

Form: Slightly larger than feral pigeon, with smaller head, larger body, and broad, rounded wings; plumage pink-white; duskier on upper back, belly, flanks, and undertail; rest of upperparts and wings dark chocolate-brown; primary flight feathers darker; lower back and rump blue-gray; uppertail coverts and tail red-orange or chestnut; eyes surrounded by red ring of bare skin with white or pale-yellow iris; bill red at base with a yellow or creamy tip; red feet

Diet: Wide variety of fruit and berries as well as leaves and flowers

Breeding: Nest is platform of twigs; 2 white eggs incubated for 13–18 days; young fledge in about 20 days

Related endangered species: Sixty-one species of pigeons are threatened, including 17 other species in the genus *Columba:* silvery wood pigeon (*C. argentina*) CR; yellow-legged pigeon (*C. pallidiceps*) EN; white-tailed laurel pigeon (*C. junoniae*) VU; maroon pigeon (*C. thomensis*) VU; and Sri Lanka wood pigeon (*C. torringtoni*) VU

Status: IUCN EN; not listed by CITES

include restoring habitat, controlling introduced predators and guarding nests to prevent predation, rescuing eggs and young from failing nests, providing the birds with extra food, and controlling disease.

The rescue program came barely in time to save the pink pigeon. The intensive management has seen a dramatic increase in the numbers of the pigeons. A few more years of decline and the species would probably have suffered the same fate as its closest relative, the long-extinct Réunion pigeon.

The pink pigeon has undergone a remarkable improvement in status. Once classified by the IUCN as Critically Endangered, it is now listed as Endangered and will shortly be downgraded to Vulnerable.

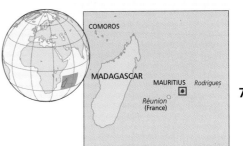

Pigeon, Victoria Crowned

Goura victoria

Among the largest of all the world's pigeons, the Victoria crowned pigeon is threatened by hunting for food and feathers. The birds are especially vulnerable since they are remarkably tame.

The Victoria crowned pigeon is one of three very closely related species of giant pigeon found on the island of New Guinea; the other two are the southern crowned pigeon and the western crowned pigeon. True to their names, the birds have a "crown"—a fanlike crest of lacy feathers.

The Victoria crowned pigeon occurs on both Papua, a province of Indonesia, and Papua New Guinea, as well as on the Indonesian islands of Biak-Supiori (where it may have been introduced) and Yapen. It breeds with the western and southern crowned pigeons in places where they occur together in the northwest of the island. The reason for its absence between Astrolabe Bay and Collingwood Bay is not known. It could be that it has never occurred there, or that it did but has been wiped out at some time in the past.

Prized as Food

As plump as a turkey, the Victoria crowned pigeon has long been prized as food by local hunters, since each bird provides plenty of succulent meat. The birds are hunted, and young are taken from the nests to rear for food. Some birds are also still killed for their beautiful crown feathers, which are used in traditional headdresses. Trapping of the birds for the aviary trade may also pose a significant threat.

With modern firearms replacing the bow and arrow and the snare, the birds are much easier to kill, although their tameness is legendary—at least in regions where they have not been heavily exploited. When approached, a pigeon will often run away. If it does not make good its escape that way, it flies up with a loud beating of its broad wings to perch awkwardly on a nearby low branch of a tree in the forest understory, peering with curiosity at its pursuer. Such a large, static target is not difficult to hit.

DATA PANEL

Victoria crowned pigeon (Victoria goura, white-tipped goura/crowned pigeon)

Goura victoria

Family: Columbidae

World population: 2,500–10,000 birds

Distribution: Parts of northern New Guinea (in both Papua and Papua New Guinea); islands of Biak-Supiori and Yapen

Habitat: Lowland forest, mainly at lowest altitudes

Size: Length: 29 in (74 cm)

Form: Huge, plump pigeon with large crest of white-tipped feathers; plumage generally bluish gray with broad, pale-gray bar in front of narrow, dark-maroon bar on each wing; pale-gray band at end of tail; large maroon area on breast; eyes have red irises; bill dark gray, paler at tip; legs and feet purplish red

Diet: Mainly berries and other fruit; seeds that have fallen to the ground

Breeding: Builds a neat, compact nest of stems, leaves, and sticks; birds in captivity begin breeding from the age of 15 months; lays single white egg and cares for fledgling for several months after hatching

Related endangered species: Western crowned pigeon (*Goura cristata*) VU; southern crowned pigeon (*G. scheepmakeri*) VU

Status: IUCN VU; CITES II

See also: The Feather Trade **1:** 46; Education **1:** 94; Pigeon, Pink **7:** 70

Threats from Logging

Victoria crowned pigeons are exclusively forest dwellers. Although they have sometimes been found as high up as 1,970 feet (600 m), they prefer forests at much lower altitudes, particularly those on flat terrain. Unfortunately, these are often just the type of forests that are threatened by logging. As well as causing immediate damage to the pigeons' forest habitat, the building of roads into the forests for logging vehicles also helps hunters gain access to the areas where the birds live.

Cause for Concern

Hunting has wiped out local populations around some villages, with birds surviving only in remote forests. In some places in Papua where settlers have moved in from other places, the species has disappeared from areas where it had previously survived regular hunting by the local people.

Although the size of its population is unknown, the Victoria crowned pigeon has been given Vulnerable status by the IUCN because conservationists think that it may be relatively rare and is declining rapidly, largely as a result of hunting. However, the Victoria crowned pigeon remains common in some more remote, undisturbed areas of forest. New information on its population size and the success of future conservation initiatives will perhaps enable its Vulnerable status to be revised.

The species is protected by law in Papua New Guinea. There are plans for various research and education programs, which will include making people aware of the need to reduce hunting. Other aims are to establish new protected areas in lowland forests and to enforce protection in those areas that are already set aside as reserves.

The Victoria crowned pigeon *has sturdy legs and feet adapted for a life spent mainly on the ground. However, the birds can fly well and perch and roost in trees.*

73

Pika, Steppe

Ochotona pusilla

The decline of the steppe pika is a long-term trend dating back to the early days of agriculture. The main cause of the decline is habitat loss.

Pikas are short-eared cousins of rabbits and hares, and in some parts of the world they can be exceedingly common. They are well suited to life in a harsh climate; their short legs, small, rounded ears, thick fur, and furry feet are all adaptations to the cold weather. They can survive long winters under deep snow, where they remain active in networks of hidden tunnels.

Being snowbound for several months obviously restricts the pikas' foraging options, so over the summer they spend much of their time preparing for the winter by collecting as much extra food as possible. Grass and leaves are harvested, allowed to dry in the sun, and gathered together in haystacks. A single pika can gather several pounds of winter fodder in one stack; and while this in itself is not enough to support the animal through the winter, it provides an essential supplement to the meager winter rations.

Decline in Numbers

Over two-thirds of the world's 26 pika species are currently threatened with extinction in the wild. One of the most notable declines has been that of the Russian steppe pika, in spite of the fact that pika populations have a quite extraordinary capacity for growth under the right conditions. A single female steppe pika can easily produce five litters of 10 babies each in a season. Assuming that half of them are females (that mature within one month and soon begin to breed themselves), by the onset of winter the family could include over 1,000 animals, every one a child or grandchild of the original female. In a good season even the first-born grandchildren may breed, in which case the potential for growth reaches staggering proportions.

However, as the proverb says, "What goes up must come down," and pika populations can disappear even faster than they build up. Populations of the Russian steppe pika vary between 0.04 and 33 animals per acre (0.1 and 80 animals per ha). These

DATA PANEL

Steppe pika

Ochotona pusilla

Family: Ochotonidae

World population: Unknown, but declining rapidly

Distribution: Steppes of Russia and Kazakhstan, between Volga and Irtysh Rivers

Habitat: Open plains, deserts, and dry grasslands

Size: Length: 5–12 in (12.5–30 cm). Weight: 4.5–14 oz (125–400 g)

Form: Dumpy, grayish-brown animal resembling small, round-eared rabbit with no visible tail and short legs; thick, dense fur

Diet: Plant material, including leaves of grasses, sedges, and herbs; also twigs and flowers of woody plants

Breeding: Between 3 and 5 litters of 3–13 young born throughout spring and summer, after gestation period of about 1 month; young mature at 1 month. Life span more than 5 years in the wild

Related endangered species: Helan Shan pika (*Ochotona helanshanensis*) CR; Koslov's pika (*O. koslowi*) EN

Status: IUCN VU; not listed by CITES

See also: Boom and Bust 1: 21; Habitat Loss 1: 38; Prairie Dog, Black-Tailed 7: 92; Souslik, European 9: 18

wild fluctuations are perfectly natural, and in a stable environment there are usually enough survivors of a crash to reestablish the population. Cycles of boom and bust restrict the genetic variability of a population, however, and the problem becomes especially acute when pika populations are isolated by farmland or other human developments. Reduced variability makes small, postcrash populations even more vulnerable to local catastrophes, be they natural (fire, drought, disease, or hard winters) or persecution by humans (especially by poisoning). Pikas need grass and other vegetation to support their large numbers, but it is destroyed along with their burrows when land is plowed up. As farmland increasingly dominates the landscape, the pikas lose out.

Crop Raiders

Changes in land use during the Middle Ages drove the steppe pikas out of large parts of their former range in what is now the Ukraine. The western part of the pika's range continued to be eroded in the following centuries, and by the early 19th century there were no pikas west of the Volga River. The remaining populations are fragmented and at risk of being poisoned, snared, or shot. Their habitat is disappearing under farmland, leaving the pikas little choice but to raid crops, provoking the hatred of farmers and plantation owners. The tender saplings of newly planted conifer plantations make easy pickings during the winter, when the trees are buried in the snow and the pikas can feed without being seen. The extent of their attacks on the trees becomes all too evident when the snow melts, but then it is too late to act, and the trees die. The frustration of landowners on finding their crops nibbled and ruined after the spring thaw is understandable. As long as humans and pikas compete for a living on the steppes, the future of this hardy and naturally prolific little animal is at risk.

Pikas *(below), also called mouse hares, are small, rabbitlike creatures that are found in parts of western North America, Asia, and eastern Europe. The steppe pika (above) occurs in the steppes of Russia and Kazakhstan.*

Pirarucu

Arapaima gigas

Information about the pirarucu, or arapaima, is too limited to establish whether or not it is an endangered species. It has been listed as Vulnerable, Insufficiently Known, and Data Deficient.

The pirarucu, or arapaima, is one of the largest freshwater fish in the world; it is generally about 10 feet (3 m) long. Its listing as an endangered species depends on when the assessment was made. Older statements usually refer to categories of greater endangeredness, owing perhaps to a cautionary approach in the face of lack of data. Some more recent reports state even higher levels of threat, probably as a result of authors quoting older literature without being aware of the latest thinking on the status of the species.

Over the past few years it has become apparent that the pirarucu is not quite as rare as it was once assumed to be, at least in some areas. However, its numbers are not known, partly because of its large geographical range and the immense size of some of the watercourses where it is found—the Amazon basin, for example. Some of its habitats are also remote and inaccessible. What is clear is that catches in areas near human communities have dropped significantly over recent years, probably indicating extinction in some regions.

Fascinating Giant

The pirarucu belongs to the family Osteoglossidae, the bonytongues. The name refers to the rough surface of the tongue—a feature that the pirarucu shares with the dragon fish. It allows the fish to grasp and chew items such as hard-scaled catfish, which many other predators are unable to handle. The body scales of the pirarucu are also hard and rough—so much so that when dried out, they can be used as sandpaper!

Being such a large fish, the pirarucu's need for oxygen is high. Yet its native waters are sometimes deficient in this vitally important component. The pirarucu holds the solution to the potentially life-threatening situation in its air bladder, which—in addition to its gills—is capable of absorbing oxygen through its blood supply and transporting it throughout the body. With so little dissolved oxygen in the water, the only alternative (and rich) source available is in the air above the water's surface. Pirarucus therefore take huge gulps of air and pass them down into the air bladder.

Perhaps the most fascinating aspect of the pirarucu's biology is its reproductive strategy. Unlike so many other large species, which shed hundreds of thousands, even millions, of eggs, an adult female pirarucu produces only about 4,000. Once fertilized, they are picked up by one of the parents in its mouth, where they are incubated until they hatch. The brooding parent also develops white pimplelike growths (tubercles) around its snout. It is thought that they secrete nutritious substances for

See also: Categories of Threat **1:** 14; Dragon Fish **4:** 36

the fry (baby fish) to feed on during their earliest days. Other fish, including freshwater angelfish, use a similar strategy.

Threats and Recovery

The pirarucu is probably threatened by pollution as a result of mining activities along rivers. Deforestation—leading to erosion, silting, and deterioration in water quality—is also a threat. Excessive fishing is another hazard in habitats that are accessible from human settlements; pirarucus are in demand as food.

The popularity of pirarucus for home aquaria has never been great, owing to their size. However, recent advances in aquarium technology have made the keeping of so-called "tank busters" more viable.

There are now several commercial breeding and rearing enterprises in parts of the pirarucu's range, producing many thousands of captive-bred specimens annually. Most of these are for food, but they could also cater to a demand from aquarists in the future.

The pirarucu *has primitive characteristics such as a flat head; ancient fossils have been found that resemble the fish.*

Pitta, Gurney's

Pitta gurneyi

Forest clearance in Thailand has caused a catastrophic decline in numbers of Gurney's pitta, reducing it to a tiny population. As a result, the spectacular bird is at risk of becoming extinct.

In the early evening of June 14, 1986, two naturalists, Philip Round and Uthai Treesucon, turned a corner on a forest trail in southern Thailand and made ornithological history. The beautiful, multicolored bird that crossed the path just in front of them was the first Gurney's pitta to have been seen in the wild for 36 years. For the two men it was the culmination of a four-year search.

The species, which was first described in 1875, was once found in semievergreen rain forests over much of central peninsular Thailand and on the island of Phuket offshore, as well as at the southern tip of

Tenasserim Province in neighboring Myanmar (Burma). Within this restricted range the bird—the only one endemic to the region—was relatively numerous at least until the early 1920s and in some areas may have been the commonest pitta species.

A Final Foothold

As a result of the rapid expansion of Thailand's human population over the 20th century, however, the country's lowland forests have been extensively felled for timber and cleared for the cultivation of fruit, coffee, rubber, and oil palm. Gurney's pitta had disappeared from southern Myanmar by 1914, and its numbers have been drastically reduced in Thailand.

By 1987 it was estimated that less than 7.7 to 19 square miles (20 to 50 sq. km) of original lowland native forest remained in Thailand. Since then this remnant has been further diminished, imprisoning Gurney's pitta in increasingly few fragments of its former range.

Even at the time of the pitta's dramatic rediscovery the remaining uncleared forest patches were rapidly being degraded or destroyed by illegal clearing to make way for rubber and oil palm plantations. At the same time, the birds were subjected to intensive hunting and trapping to feed Thailand's illegal but thriving trade in wild birds.

A further year of such assaults might have wiped the species out, but the rediscovery set conservationists in action. A survey of the Khao Nor Chuchi area where it had been spotted suggested that the region might contain about 40 pairs of the

DATA PANEL

Gurney's pitta (black-breasted pitta)

Pitta gurneyi

Family: Pittidae

World population: 24 birds in 2000

Distribution: Now at just 1 site (Khao Nor Chuchi Wildlife Sanctuary) in southern Thailand; once widespread in Thailand and also found in Myanmar (Burma)

Habitat: Secondary, regenerating, lowland semievergreen forest, mainly below 500 ft (150 m)

Size: Length: 8 in (20 cm). Weight: 2–3 oz (60–90 g)

Form: Sturdy-bodied, large-headed, short-tailed bird with upright posture and strong, longish legs. Male has black forecrown and dark-blue nape; also dark reddish-brown wings and upperparts, yellow and black underparts, and deep-blue tail. Female has reddish-brown upperparts and blue tail, but shows buffy-brown crown and nape, blackish-brown eyepatch, whitish throat, and buff underparts with fine black barring

Diet: Worms, insects and insect larvae, snails, slugs, and other small animals

Breeding: Wet season, April–October; nest a dome of dead leaves and small sticks on a base of slightly larger sticks; inner cup for eggs is lined with fine, black rootlets; usually 3–4 eggs are laid and incubated by both sexes for an unknown period, but probably 10–14 days; young fledge at 14–15 days

Related endangered species: Nine species of pitta are threatened, including the superb pitta (*Pitta superba*) VU; whiskered pitta (*P. kochi*) VU; and fairy pitta (*P. nympha*) VU

Status: IUCN CR; CITES I

pittas. In addition, researchers found at least four smaller populations in neighboring forests, all of which have since disappeared.

In 1987 the Thai government declared part of Khao Nor Chuchi a Nonhunting Area. Unfortunately for the pitta, most of the lowland forest in which it lives was excluded from protection. Despite the upgrading of the area to Wildlife Sanctuary status in 1993, it remains vulnerable to the threats of habitat destruction and illegal trapping for the cage-bird trade, and still excludes key habitat.

Conservation Efforts

From modest beginnings in the 1980s the work of saving Gurney's pitta grew into a large-scale international conservation program. From 1990 the Khao Nor Chuchi Lowland Forest Project spent hundreds of thousands of dollars on demarcating the protected area, mapping the forest, and training staff. The plan was also to involve local people in management and education activities intended to reduce pressures that were fueling trapping and forest clearance. However, this was never implemented, since the benefits would have been too small and unlikely to be evenly distributed. A sustainable agro-forestry initiative, involving the distribution of 160,000 seedlings, promoted species diversity by encouraging settlers to grow other crops besides the rubber trees and oil palms that threaten to take over the area. Other projects included helping villagers establish fish ponds and the building of a village hall.

Despite these efforts, the project has had only limited success. The Thai government's Royal Forest Department has ignored encroachments into the sanctuary, including the invasion of a clearing where one of the last pairs of pittas lived. Meanwhile, prices for rubber and palm oil have fallen, and settlers have tried to compensate by planting fresh trees, destroying yet more forest in the process. Another problem has been that the settlers include recent immigrants to the area, making community-based work more difficult.

Gurney's pitta
boasts spectacular plumage, making it
irresistible to trappers who supply the cage-bird trade.

Besides applying pressure on the Thai government, conservationists are now eager to search for any remaining Gurney's pitta populations in southern Myanmar—no easy task given the political situation in that country—and to improve protection for the beleaguered Thai population. Time is not on the birds' side, however: Only 11 pairs and 2 unpaired males were found during the last breeding season, and at least one nest had suffered predation by a snake.

79

Platy, Cuatro Ciénegas

Xiphophorus gordoni

Since their introduction during the first decade of the 20th century countless millions of platies have been bred in captivity specifically for aquarists. As a result, numerous color and fin varieties and other hybrids have been created all over the world. While at least three species are relatively secure, other species are close to extinction.

The Cuatro Ciénegas, or northern, platy is a species from the northern edge of the platy's distribution range. It is, in fact, one of three closely related species that are believed to have evolved from a common ancestor. Like its two closest relatives, the Monterrey platy and the Muzquiz platy (officially described as recently as 1988), the species occurs in a small, isolated area. The continued survival of all three species is at risk.

The Cuatro Ciénegas basin (its name translates as "four marshes") is located roughly in the center of the northern Mexican state of Coahuila. It is surrounded on three sides (east, north, and west) by mountains.

Over geological time, as the mountains slowly rose up, erosion and other geological processes began to generate sediment. The sediment built up and eventually formed barriers near the open (southern) end of the basin. This effectively sealed off the basin from the outside world.

Gradually, subterranean water erosion and the subsequent subsidence of the roofs of some of the underground watercourses led to the formation of the series of springs, sinkholes, marshes, and other bodies of water that characterize the Cuatro Ciénegas Basin. Some of the aquatic habitats are known to have been isolated from each other for many thousands of years, providing ideal conditions for the evolution of species found nowhere else (some 10 species are, in fact, known to be endemic—or native—to the basin).

Restricted Range and Threats

Owing to its special characteristics, the Cuatro Ciénegas Basin has been the focus of intense study ever since its isolated and unique fauna were

DATA PANEL

Cuatro Ciénegas platy (northern platy)

Xiphophorus gordoni

Family: Poeciliidae

World population: Unknown, but rare within its total range; common in restricted stretches of water

Distribution: Laguna Santa Tecla in the Cuatro Ciénegas Basin, Coahuila, Mexico

Habitat: Shallow, alkaline, vegetated springs; marshy areas associated with the lake

Size: Length: male up to 1.4 in (3.5 cm); female up to 1.6 in (4 cm)

Form: Body has overall blue sheen; brown on back, silvery white on belly; the 2 zones are separated by a dark zigzag line that runs from gill cover to caudal peduncle (base of tail). Both sexes have black blotch (gravid spot) around vent (cavity into which alimentary canal, genital, and urinary ducts open). Male has anal fin modified into elongated copulatory (mating) organ known as the gonopodium. Dorsal (back) fin has two dark crescents separated by brownish-gold band

Diet: Algae, other plant material, debris, and small aquatic invertebrates

Breeding: Female stores sperm following internal insemination via male's gonopodium and fertilizes series of egg batches. Fertilized eggs retained by female in ovarian follicles (egg sacs) until they hatch. Female gives birth to about 20 fully formed young. Broods produced on monthly basis through year

Related endangered species: Monterrey platy (*Xiphophorus couchianus*) CR; Muzquiz platy (*X. meyeri*) EN

Status: IUCN EN; not listed by CITES

See also: Speciation **1:** 26; Goodeid, Gold Sawfin **5:** 36; Pupfish, Devil's Hole **7:** 94

The Cuatro Ciénegas platy

(above) lives in the springs feeding a single lake in Mexico and is Endangered. The related Monterrey platy (inset) is Critically Endangered.

discovered in 1939. The Cuatro Ciénegas platy was discovered in 1961 in the southeastern corner of the basin and named after the nearest town. Subsequent studies revealed that the species was restricted to springs feeding into Laguna Santa Tecla and marshy outflows associated with the lake. Further searches carried out since then have failed to yield any additional specimens elsewhere in the basin. Such a restricted distribution immediately places a species under threat of extinction. A single major event—induced naturally or by humans—could wipe out the whole population at a stroke.

The Cuatro Ciénegas platy faces several major threats to its survival. At the top end of its range the sources of the springs have been enlarged and channeled in order to increase the flow of water. The species prefers heavily vegetated water that is less than 10 inches (25 cm) in depth, but the water flow changes have altered the environmental conditions and hence the vegetation within the basin. Farther down the range pools fed by the springs have also been significantly altered. Some have even been connected to each other for irrigation purposes.

Water quality has deteriorated too as a result of an influx of pollution generated by people. Habitat destruction by cattle and the establishment of the water hyacinth—a fast-spreading weed—are further threats to the platy's existence.

Conservation Measures

In order to save its species from impending extinction, a reserve was established in the Cuatro Ciénegas Basin in 1994, incorporating some of the habitats occupied by the platy. The reserve appears to offer the species some degree of protection, but the full benefits are yet to be seen. Many of the measures are still at the proposal stage or yet to be implemented.

In the meantime the platy's continued survival is dependent on populations that are being bred and maintained in captivity in countries such as the United States, Britain, and Germany.

Platypus

Ornithorhynchus anatinus

Platypuses are no longer hunted for their fur, but they face threats from pollution and the environmental consequences of modern development. The platypus has become a well-known conservation symbol for its freshwater habitat of southeastern Australia.

European settlers in Australia first saw and described the duck-billed platypus in 1797, but it was another hundred years before the animal's unique anatomy and reproductive habits were scientifically studied. In the past the platypus was hunted extensively for its fur, which, like that of other aquatic mammals, is extremely dense, so it keeps the animal warm even when wet. Thousands of platypuses were killed for their skins, while the heads and bills were sold as curios.

Hunting has all but exterminated the platypus population of South Australia: The last sighting of the animals on the lower Murray River, one of Australia's major rivers, was as long ago as 1960. The only platypuses living in the state these days are an introduced population on Kangaroo Island off South Australia and a few animals in captivity. Today wild platypuses still occasionally come across the border from New South Wales.

People are not the only predators to have taken a serious toll. In the days before European settlement the only predator of the platypus was the native Australian water rat. In recent times, however, introduced foxes, cats, rats, and dogs have all killed platypuses, especially young ones. Road deaths are also becoming a problem in urban areas.

The Costs of Development

The main problems facing platypuses today are those associated with modern development. Pollution and physical changes threaten the waters where they live. Many rivers have become unsuitable for platypuses through dramatically altered rates of flow as a result of the diversion of water for human use. Artificial structures such as weirs, drains, dams, and grilles built

AUSTRALIA

DATA PANEL

Platypus (duck-billed platypus)

Ornithorhynchus anatinus

Family: Ornithorhynchidae

World population: Unknown; low thousands

Distribution: Fresh waters of eastern Australia; throughout Tasmania and King Island in the Bass Strait; introduced population on Kangaroo Island off South Australia

Habitat: Freshwater rivers, lakes, and lagoons

Size: Length: 12–22 in (30–55 cm); males up to 20% bigger than females on mainland, but in Tasmania the sexes are similarly sized. Weight: 1–5.5 lb (0.5–2.5 kg)

Form: Unlike any other mammal; body is robust and slightly flattened, covered in dense, brown fur; legs short, feet large and webbed; tail flattened from above and paddlelike; head dominated by large, soft, rubbery beak, eyes small, ears hidden in fur; male has prominent sharp spurs on hind feet

Diet: Mostly freshwater crustaceans, worms, and insect larvae; some small fish and frogs

Breeding: One to 3 (usually 2) sticky-shelled eggs laid August–October after 2-week gestation; incubated by mother for further 2 weeks before hatching; young feed on milk from ducts on mother's belly; weaned at 4–5 months; mature at 2 years. Life span up to 15 years in the wild

Related endangered species: No close relatives

Status: Not listed by IUCN; not listed by CITES

See also: Communities and Ecosystems 1: 22; Pollution 1: 50; Echidna, Long-Beaked 4: 60

The platypus's bill *is not really like that of a duck. Soft and leathery, it is well supplied with nerve endings. When hunting underwater, the platypus keeps its eyes closed and "feels" its way around with the bill, which can even sense electrical activity in the nerves of invertebrate prey.*

across rivers to trap debris can make it difficult for platypuses to travel far.

Pollution is a problem for all freshwater animals. The particular threat for the platypus is that the fine, dense fur that it relies on for warmth underwater can be fouled by waste chemicals, while detergents in the water may destroy the natural oils that keep it waterproof. An adult platypus eats a great deal—up to half its own body weight every night—so anything that affects its food soon has a carry-over effect on platypus numbers. For example, nutrient enrichment by fertilizers washed off farmland may seem like the opposite of poisoning, but ultimately it is just as damaging. In a process known as "eutrophication" sudden blooms of algae—caused by the extra nutrients—can quickly choke a river or lake, using up all the available oxygen so that other plants and invertebrates cannot survive. It is also the case that some kinds of blue-green algae are highly toxic and can kill even quite large animals.

Studies of the platypus in captivity are allowing a better understanding of the problems it faces in the wild. For example, recent studies in South Australia—aimed at improving the success of captive-breeding programs—highlighted the importance of maintaining the natural chemical balance of the platypus's remaining wild habitat. Before 1990 only one platypus had ever been produced in captivity. As a result of the captive research it is now clear that factors such as the relative acidity of the water play a crucial role in breeding success.

The platypus is a popular animal that attracts much public attention. As such, it is a fine example of a "flagship species." Conservation measures designed to help it also benefit the rest of the ecosystem in which it lives. What is good for the platypus turns out to be helpful for less publicized aquatic creatures too.

Plover, Piping

Charadrius melodus

The piping plover is an energetic little shorebird. It has been threatened by human pressure on its habitat and has declined considerably since the 1950s. However, a huge effort is being made to help the bird, and if recent increases continue, it will be downlisted.

The piping plover is the rarest of the ringed and sand plovers that breed in North America. It has not fared well in the modern world. Its troubles began when hunters shot large numbers during the 19th century. From about 1850 its range contracted considerably, and by 1900 the toll taken by hunting had brought the piping plover to the verge of extinction. In the nick of time changes were introduced to the game laws, and protection allowed the species to recover considerably by the 1920s.

In more recent times the piping plover has suffered another decline, this time as a result of disturbance to its habitat by humans. The building of roads, houses, and other developments in coastland areas have all had an adverse effect on numbers.

As soon as the birds arrive on the breeding sites from their wintering grounds, human activity can interfere with the birds' ability to establish territories and their courtship. Because their eggs and young are so well camouflaged, they are easily trampled or dispersed by people visiting beaches; and if disturbance is severe, the birds may abandon attempts to breed in the area. The use of off-road vehicles on breeding beaches destroys plover nests. Pet dogs allowed to run free eat eggs, kill chicks, and frighten adults, while garbage and food scraps dumped on beaches attract other predators such as foxes, rats, possums, skunks, feral cats and dogs, and gulls.

In 1985 the piping plover was placed on the Federal list of Threatened and Endangered Species. The Great Lakes population received Endangered status, while the Great Plains and East Coast

DATA PANEL

Piping plover

Charadrius melodus

Family: Charadriidae

World population: Fewer than 3,000 pairs

Distribution: Breeds on northern Great Plains of Canada and U.S. and along Atlantic coast from Newfoundland to North (and occasionally South) Carolina; also around Great Lakes. Winters on Atlantic coasts of southern U.S.; also Bahamas, Gulf of Mexico, northwestern Mexico, and eastern Caribbean

Habitat: Great Plains breeders nest on sand and gravel shores of large, alkaline lakes; also on river banks, sand and salt flats, and

floodplains. Coastal breeders nest on sandy beaches and winter at long-used sites on sandy beaches and sand flats; sometimes on estuary mudflats and dunes

Size: Length: 6.8–7 in (17–18 cm); wingspan: 14–15 in (35–38 cm). Weight: 1.5–2.3 oz (43–64 g)

Form: Small, plump-breasted bird with orange legs; short, black bill (orange with black tip in breeding season); pale sandy-gray upperparts, white underparts; black bar across forehead and black "collar" in breeding season (both pale in winter). White rump, visible in flight, distinguishes it from more common semipalmated and snowy plovers

Diet: Aquatic invertebrates, including worms, crustaceans, mollusks, and insects; also land-dwelling insects such as flies, midges, beetles, and grasshoppers

Breeding: Female lays 3–4 dark-spotted buff eggs in April or May; incubated by both parents for about 4 weeks; chicks cared for by both parents; fledge after about 4 weeks

Related endangered species: Mountain plover (*Charadrius montanus*) VU; New Zealand dotterel (*C. obscurus*) VU; St. Helena plover (*C. sanctaehelenaei*) EN; hooded plover (*C. rubricollis*) LRnt

Status: IUCN VU; not listed by CITES

See also: Pollution **1:** 50; Research **1:** 84; Curlew, Eskimo **3:** 84

The piping plover *breeds in the United States and Canada and has a winter range that extends from North Carolina south to Jamaica and northern Mexico.*

populations were listed as Threatened. A recovery plan was approved in 1988. As a result of various conservation measures, numbers are now stable or increasing, particularly along parts of the Atlantic coast, and especially in New England.

International censuses of the piping plover involving eight countries are carried out every five years for wintering and breeding populations. The breeding census shows that the Atlantic coast populations are faring much better than those in the interior of the United States and Canada. In the northern Great Plains breeding numbers are decreasing every year as a result of drought and flooding, often caused by water-management projects. In the Great Lakes area there is a viable breeding population in only one state—Michigan.

The Great Lakes birds may suffer from high levels of toxic pollutants, especially PCBs (polychlorinated biphenols). Piping plovers, especially males, are extremely loyal to breeding sites, returning year after year, so it is a serious loss if a particular site is damaged or destroyed.

Since the piping plover spends as much as 70 to 80 percent of its annual cycle away from its breeding range, it is vital to protect its wintering habitat, too. Conservationists are focusing attention on the Laguna Madre region of Texas and Mexico, where there are vast areas of winter habitat. Such wilderness, also susceptible to development, could save many piping plovers and other endangered birds. Other threats that need constant vigilance are oil spills and dredging operations in the Gulf of Mexico.

85

Porpoise, Harbor

Phocoena phocoena

The harbor porpoise is also known as the common porpoise, a name that was justified until fairly recently. Now there are fears that centuries of hunting and environmental damage are taking their toll.

Porpoises are cetaceans—aquatic mammals with no hind limbs and a blowhole for breathing. Porpoises and dolphins have not received anything like the same attention as larger cetaceans, such as great whales. However, they are subjected to the same pressures—namely, hunting, accidental killing, habitat loss, declining food resources, and pollution. Porpoise numbers have undergone a dramatic decline in the 20th century, and some populations, in the Mediterranean for example, are already virtually extinct. The loss of harbor porpoises from the Mediterranean means that the population in the Black Sea is now extremely isolated.

In the early part of the 20th century there were 30,000 harbor porpoises in the Black Sea, but fisheries in Turkey, Bulgaria, Romania, and the former Soviet Union reduced the numbers to dangerously low levels, with an annual catch of about 2,500 porpoises. The Bulgarian, Romanian, and Russian fisheries stopped hunting porpoises in 1966, and the Turks followed suit in 1983; porpoise numbers in the Black Sea have since rallied to about 10,000 individuals.

Declining Populations

Elsewhere there are larger populations, notably the 100,000 or so porpoises that live in the North Sea, and the 50,000 to 70,000 that occupy the waters west of Greenland as far south as the Gulf of Maine. Intensive hunting and accidental killing by the United States, Canadian, and especially Danish fisheries inflict a death toll somewhere in the region of 10,000 porpoises per year. Denmark also persists in hunting porpoises in the Baltic, where the annual catch of about 3,000 animals is not sustainable. There is also evidence that porpoises are being regularly affected by pollution and disease.

International restrictions on hunting would certainly help the harbor porpoise; but further action is also needed to prevent accidents caused by

DATA PANEL

Harbor porpoise (common porpoise)

Phocoena phocoena

Family: Phocoenidae

World population: About 250,000

Distribution: North Atlantic, North Pacific, Arctic oceans, and some adjoining seas; isolated population in the Black Sea

Habitat: Shallow coasts and estuaries in cool, temperate waters

Size: Length: 4–6 ft (120–190 cm). Weight: 100–132 lb (45–60 kg); up to 198 lb (90 kg)

Form: Stout dolphin with blunt, conical snout and triangular dorsal fin; dark gray skin above, fading to almost white on belly

Diet: Schooling fish (cod, pollack, herring, hake, salmon, and sardines); also squid and shrimps

Breeding: Single calf born May–August after 11-month gestation; weaned at 8 months. Life span up to 14 years

Related endangered species: Gulf of California porpoise (*Phocoena sinus*) CR; Burmeister's porpoise (*P. spinipinnis*) DD

Status: IUCN VU; CITES II

See also: Populations **1:** 20; Hunting **1:** 42; Whale, Killer **10:** 48; Whale, White **10:** 58

Harbor porpoises *are not nearly as active at the surface as other dolphins. Most sightings consist of the animal's back and dorsal fin rolling forward in the water.*

fishing nets and tackle, which kill thousands of porpoises a year. Unfortunately, porpoises and humans frequently compete directly for the same fish in the same waters, so fishermen rarely have sympathy for their victims. There are ways of reducing the risk to porpoises—by equipping nets with acoustic "pingers" to warn them away, for example. However, such equipment is expensive, and fishermen are unwilling to spend money on protecting a species that they believe is already costing them a fortune in lost fish.

Shy and Retiring
Recent research in Scotland has revealed that harbor porpoises have another enemy in the form of the bottlenose dolphin. Many local porpoises bear serious scars caused by dolphin teeth, and mortal wounding is apparently not uncommon. As yet the full reasons for

this unusual aggression between species are not understood. Porpoises also frequently fall prey to sharks, and these natural hazards are a possible reason for their wary behavior.

While their coastal preferences mean that porpoises are often spotted from land or from boats, they are almost impossible to approach and certainly never come to meet boats or to ride bow-waves in the same way that dolphins do. Shy animals, they are not as spectacular as the great whales and are less acrobatic than most dolphins.

The retiring nature of harbor porpoises is probably one reason why the efforts to protect them have not captured the public imagination. However, these animals are highly intelligent; they are becoming increasingly endangered, and they are certainly worthy of further conservation efforts.

Possum, Leadbeater's

Gymnobelideus leadbeateri

A long-lost animal whose particular habitat and lifestyle requirements have already given it one brush with extinction, Leadbeater's possum is now threatened again and in need of radical conservation measures to keep it from disappearing forever.

Leadbeater's possum was first described in 1867. It was extremely rare, and because of its nocturnal habits and largely inaccessible habitat only four more specimens were caught before 1921, when it was declared extinct. Most of its biology was still a mystery.

Leadbeater's possums were scarce in the 19th century for two main reasons. First, they have quite specific habitat requirements, and suitable homes were few and far between. These nimble marsupials only live in well-developed forests containing a tall species of eucalyptus known as mountain ash. They are completely dependent on an adequate supply of old, hollow trees in which to nest, and they need plenty of nearby wattle acacia scrub in which to feed. This combination was only available in a few limited areas of Victoria in southern Australia.

The second threat was competition from other better adapted possums, particularly the sugar glider.

Changes in climate and vegetation types over the last two million years have shifted conditions in favor of the sugar gliders, which can "fly" between widely separated trees. The nongliding Leadbeater's possum can only jump comparatively short distances. The overall picture in the late 19th century was of a species whose time was up, and for once the decline appeared to have nothing to do with humans.

Rising from the Ashes

In 1939, 30 years after the last Leadbeater's possum was recorded, a devastating wildfire tore through the central highlands, destroying about 70 percent of the state of Victoria's forests. The fire was catastrophic, but while large areas of burned-out habitat were cleared, the rest began a steady regeneration. Dense scrub sprang up from the ashes, and new trees began to

AUSTRALIA
New South Wales
Victoria
Tasmania

DATA PANEL

Leadbeater's possum

Gymnobelideus leadbeateri

Family: Petauridae

World population: About 5,000 in 1992; may be considerably fewer now

Distribution: Central highlands of Victoria, Australia

Habitat: Australian mountain ash forest with dense undergrowth of wattle acacia

Size: Length head/body: up to 6 in (15 cm); tail: 6 in (15 cm). Weight: 2.5–6 oz (70–170 g)

Form: Guinea-pig-sized marsupial with long, furry tail, covered in thick, velvety-gray fur with dark stripe down back; eyes very large and black; female's pouch opens at front

Diet: Mostly insects; also sap, gum, and honeydew

Breeding: One or 2 young born at any time of year except midsummer; weaned at 3 months; mature at 2 years. Life span unknown, but probably about 5 years

Related endangered species: Mahogany glider *(Petaurus gracilis)* * EN; Tate's triok *(Dactilopsila tatei)* EN

Status: IUCN EN; not listed by CITES

See also: Specialization 1: 28; Natural Extinction 1: 34; Glider, Mahogany 5: 32; Pygmy-Possum, Mountain 8: 4

grow around the blackened trunks. After 20 years or so, and without anyone realizing it, huge tracts of habitat ideal for Leadbeater's possum were re-created. The standing dead wood left by the 1939 fire provided an abundance of nesting sites, while the fresh new growth yielded plenty of the gummy sap and hidden insects on which the possums could feed. From some secret refuge the species recovered, taking full advantage of this unexpected second chance. In 1961 a Leadbeater's possum—only the sixth specimen ever recorded—was spotted by delighted members of a local wildlife group.

By the mid-1980s there were an estimated 5,000 Leadbeater's possums living in Victoria, and extensive studies had revealed all kinds of fascinating facts about their biology. For example, unlike most mammals, it is the female that stakes out the breeding territory, aided by a faithful male and several of her sons. Female youngsters are driven away as soon as they reach maturity.

Short-Lived Success?

This was new and exciting information, but at the same time, other studies on the possums' new habitat suggested that their recovery would be short-lived. The old dead trees in which the possums live are collapsing at a rapid rate; and because the rest of the trees in the forest are still young, it will probably be over 100 years before the dead wood is replaced. In many areas the new forest has already begun to be logged. Zoologists predict that the Leadbeater's possum population is destined to decline by about 90 percent in the early years of the 21st century.

Radical new forest-management plans are now being put in place to conserve the species in nature reserves, and the Australian government is under pressure to adopt possum-friendly logging practices in the state-owned forests that have become the refuge of these intriguing mammals.

Leadbeater's possum *is considered a relatively primitive species. It lacks many of the specializations shown by other possums, such as an elongated finger for extracting insects from under bark or a web of skin between its front and hind limbs that can be used for gliding.*

Potoroo, Long-Footed

Potorous longipes

One of the world's most recently described mammals, the long-footed potoroo is among Australia's rarest animals. Living in the dense undergrowth of wet forests, these tiny kangaroos try to avoid predators such as domestic dogs. Now inroads are being made into even their most remote refuges.

The long-footed potoroo is the rarest of the three surviving species of potoroo, or rat kangaroo, as they are sometimes known. Potoroos are marsupials and have pouches, but they are not as large as kangaroos: All are about the size of a rabbit, or smaller.

The long-footed potoroo was recognized as a distinct species as recently as 1978 and was only fully described in 1980. Such a fact may seem surprising, given that the only known colonies live in the relatively well-populated Australian states of New South Wales and Victoria. However, potoroos are extremely shy animals and live in remote areas of dense vegetation where they are rarely disturbed by people. They forage at night, eating mainly underground fungi and plant material.

Dogs, foxes, and cats had not been introduced to Australia in the centuries when the potoroos were evolving their quiet, fungus-eating way of life. Since Europeans began settling the continent, however, the domestic animals they took with them have posed a threat. Like many native Australian mammals, the potoroo is virtually defenseless against such effective predators. For a while the potoroo managed to evade extinction by retreating to the most inaccessible habitat it could find. Now, however, even the remotest hideaways are being exposed.

Nowhere to Hide

The habitats on which the potoroos rely are being spoiled as timber companies venture deeper into the forests to gain access to valuable hardwood trees. The roads built to allow the trees to be taken away carve up areas of pristine habitat and expose the insides of even very dense forests to disturbance.

The plight of the potoroo is just one of the reasons why the Australian timber industry is highly controversial. Only about 13 percent of the forest known to be home to long-footed potoroos is currently protected. The rest is all state-owned and as such can still be logged. Timber cutting in Australia is much more closely monitored than in many other countries, and there is less wholesale

DATA PANEL

Long-footed potoroo

Potorous longipes

Family: Potoroidae

World population: Unknown

Distribution: Parts of southeastern Australia

Habitat: Wet forests at altitudes of 470–2,620 ft (150–800 m) with an annual rainfall of 43–47 in (110–120 cm)

Size: Length head/body: 15–17 in (38–41.5 cm); tail: about 12.5 in (32 cm); males 20% bigger than females. Weight: 3.5–4.8 lb (1.6–2.2 kg)

Form: Rabbit-sized kangaroo with thick, gray-brown fur and elongated back feet and toes

Diet: Mostly fungi; some invertebrates and plant material

Breeding: Single young born after estimated 38-day gestation; born at any time of year, though few arrive in the fall. Two or 3 births per female per year. Young spend up to 5 months in the pouch; mature at 2 years. Longevity unknown

Related endangered species: Gilbert's potoroo (*Potorous gilbertii*) CR; northern bettong (*Bettongia tropica*) EN

Status: IUCN EN; not listed by CITES

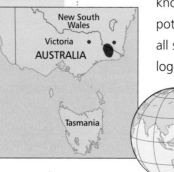

New South Wales

Victoria

AUSTRALIA

Tasmania

See also: Speciation 1: 26; Habitat Loss 1: 38; Rock-Wallaby, Prosperine 8: 36

destruction of the sort that still occurs in South America and Southeast Asia. However, once a road has been built for the transportation of timber, the interior of the forest is no longer a refuge against intruding predators.

The Fight against Extinction

Today there are three known populations of long-footed potoroo in southeastern Australia. One was discovered as recently as 1995, so there is hope that there may still be other undiscovered populations hiding away elsewhere.

A number of conservation management plans are being investigated with the aim of preserving the habitats of the long-footed potoroo and its cousin, the long-nosed potoroo. Important measures include setting up protected areas from which predators are excluded and educating the public so that any sightings of the long-footed potoroo can be reported and used to get a clearer picture of the species' distribution and numbers. As a precaution against total extinction, a small colony of long-footed potoroos is being kept in captivity at a wildlife sanctuary in Victoria.

The long-footed potoroo *hops around on its back legs and uses the front ones for digging up underground fungi to eat.*

Prairie Dog, Black-Tailed

Cynomys ludovicianus

Although not yet an endangered species, the black-tailed prairie dog has suffered huge losses and now survives mainly in protected areas. Other prairie dog species face similar but potentially more serious problems, since they never bred as quickly as their black-tailed cousins.

The prairie dog is not a dog at all, but a type of ground squirrel. It is a colonial creature that lives in large numbers in extensive burrow systems called towns. In fact, "cities" might be a better description. Early explorers described some prairie dog towns as extending for many miles and containing tens of thousands of animals. The largest town ever recorded was said to cover 25,000 square miles (65,000 sq. km) and was home to 400 million prairie dogs.

Within the towns the animals live in small social groups called coteries, each occupying about 1 acre (0.5 ha). Coteries consist of several males and females, generally close relatives, together with their offspring. They defend their part of the town against rival groups. Prairie dogs have a very complex social life, involving communication with others and complicated behavioral mechanisms to prevent inbreeding in the large colonies.

Burrow entrances are sited between carefully shaped mounds, the position of which allows a constant flow of fresh air to enter the underground tunnels. Other burrows have mounds at the entrance, providing the prairie dogs with vantage points from which they can survey their territory. From the mounds lookouts keep constant watch for danger and for trespassers. The animals often emit a loud double bark, throwing their arms into the air and arching their back as they stand upright on their hind legs. This keeps them in contact with the rest of the community. Vocal warnings alert others to the approach of predators such as coyotes and badgers. Aerial predators such as hawks and eagles are also a threat and sometimes cause the sentries to call in a slightly different way.

Making Enemies

The prairie dogs nibble down taller vegetation so as to maintain a short turf throughout their town, making it difficult for predators to approach without being seen.

DATA PANEL

Black-tailed prairie dog

Cynomys ludovicianus

Family: Sciuridae

World population: Many thousands

Distribution: Western central U.S., from Canadian to Mexican borders

Habitat: Open short-grass prairies

Size: Length head/body:11–13 in (26–31 cm), female about 10% smaller than male; tail: 3–4 in (7–9.5 cm). Weight: 20–52 oz (575–1,490 g)

Form: Short-legged ground squirrel, with sandy-brown coat and black tip to tail

Diet: Mainly grasses but also some other plants; occasionally grasshoppers

Breeding: Three to 5 young born March–April after gestation period of about 4 months. Life span about 5 years

Related endangered species: Mexican prairie dog (*Cynomys mexicanus*) EN; Utah prairie dog (*C. parvidens*) LRcd. The Arizona black-tailed praire dog subspecies (*C. l. arizonensis*) is listed as DD

Status: IUCN LRnt; not listed by CITES

See also: Life Strategies 1: 24; Habitat Loss 1: 38; Souslik, European 9: 18; Squirrel, Eurasian Red 9: 28

It also means that they destroy some of the local vegetation. Thousands of prairie dogs can eat a great deal of grass and other prairie plants, which makes them unpopular with ranchers, who see good grazing material nourishing prairie dogs instead of beef cattle. One prairie dog may not eat very much, but even quite a small town will consume as much as several cattle in a day. The many burrow entrances and shallow tunnels create a dangerous terrain for horses and their riders. Horses risk broken legs as they walk or gallop across a town, and their riders may be thrown off and seriously injured. Ranchers have gone out of their way to get rid of prairie dogs, usually using poison that is heaped into the burrows and kills large numbers of dogs cheaply and easily.

Elsewhere, the prairies have been turned into farmland. Farmers want to get rid of the prairie dogs because their burrows ensnare tractors and obstruct the planting and harvesting of crops. Deep plowing destroys the prairie dog towns anyway, and the new crops create an unsuitable environment for the animals.

Wiped Out

As a result of these pressures and thanks to government policies to protect the rangeland, prairie dogs have been wiped out over large areas. The black-tailed prairie dog is found mainly in protected areas, such as the Wind Cave National Park in South Dakota. The closely related Utah prairie dog, which was never common anyway, has disappeared from about 90 percent of its former range, and the Mexican prairie dog is now an endangered species.

Prairie dogs often stand on their hind legs to get a better view. They are always on the lookout for predators.

Pupfish, Devil's Hole

Cyprinodon diabolis

The Devil's Hole pupfish gets its name from the freshwater limestone cave pool in which it lives. Its entire life cycle is spent largely within the boundaries of a shelf near the surface of the pool. If conditions on the shelf are less than ideal, the pupfish is in immediate danger.

The Devil's Hole pupfish has been known since 1891. However, for 40 years it was assumed to be a variant of another well-known species, the desert pupfish. In 1930 its distinctive nature was fully realized, and it was named as a separate species.

The "devil" that the pupfish bears in its common name is not a reflection of its form or habits, but rather of its natural habitat: Devil's Hole cave pool in Nye County, Nevada. The narrow but deep dimensions of the pool make diving difficult for those allowed to use it (researchers and others involved in scientific work on the pool and its inhabitants). Devil's Hole is 55 feet (17 m) long, 10 feet (3 m) wide, and over 300 feet (90 m) deep. The pupfish has been found at depths of up to 80 feet (25 m). However, much of its everyday life is based around a shallow ledge or shelf measuring 18 by 10 feet (5.5 by 3 m). The Devil's Hole pupfish congregate here to spawn and to feed on the tiny aquatic invertebrates that live and feed on an algal "mat."

Life on the Shelf

The Devil's Hole pupfish lives in precarious conditions, and the Devil's Hole shelf plays a pivotal role in the survival of the species. As with other species, water level is critical; even a minor drop spells real danger for the pupfish. If the shelf were deeper within Devil's Hole, then water level fluctuations would present less of a problem. As it is, a decrease in water level of only 39 inches (100 cm) exposes the shallowest area of the shelf and destroys much of the algal growth. As a result, the invertebrate population is reduced, and the

DATA PANEL

Devil's Hole pupfish

Cyprinodon diabolis

Family: Cyprinodontidae

World population: About 650

Distribution: Devil's Hole, Ash Meadows National Wildlife Refuge, Nye County, Nevada

Habitat: Largely confined to shallow water over an algae-covered shelf; specimens also found in deeper water down to 80 ft (25 m). Water temperature about 86°F (30°C)

Size: Length: males 1 in (2.5 cm); females smaller

Form: Relatively large head; dorsal fin set well back on body; lacks pelvic (hip) fins. Males in breeding condition have bluish tinge to body and black edges to the yellowish-golden fins. At other times the body is brown with silvery sides and numerous black specks

Diet: Small, aquatic invertebrate fauna of shelf's algal mat

Breeding: Eggs laid among algae on the shallow spawning shelf from spring into summer

Related endangered species: Other Cyprinodonts, including Cachorrito lodero (*Cyprinodon beltrani*) EN; Leon Springs pupfish (*C. bovinus*) CR; Comanche Springs pupfish (*C. elegans*) EN; Perrito de carbonera (*C. fontinalis*) EN; Cachorrito cangrejero (*C. labiosus*) EN; large-scale pupfish (*C. macrolepis*) EN; Cachorrito gigante (*C. maya*) EN; Cachorrito de mezquital (*C. meeki*) CR; Cachorrito cabezon (*C. pachycephalus*) CR; Pecos pupfish (*C. pecoensis*) CR; Owen's pupfish (*C. radiosus*) EN; Cachorrito boxeador (*C. simus*) EN; Cachorrito de dorsal larga (*C. verecundus*) CR; and Cachorrito de charco azul (*C. veronicae*) CR

Status: IUCN VU; not listed by CITES

94

See also: Drainage and Irrigation **1:** 40; Research **1:** 84; Toothcarp, Valencia **9:** 80

The Devil's Hole pupfish

is believed to be the vertebrate species with the smallest natural habitat in the world. Despite the problems of its range, its future appears to be in good hands.

fish are deprived of a significant part of their food supply. A further reduction in water level, leading to exposure of the whole ledge, would cause the destruction of spawning sites. The result would be possible extinction if levels remained low for any length of time.

The Pupfish and the Law

In 1952 Devil's Hole was incorporated into the Death Valley National Monument, offering the cave pool official protection. It took 15 more years for the pupfish to be recognized as an endangered species. However, its newfound legal status, which should have been enough to ensure its continued survival, did not produce the desired results. In what is sometimes reported as a serious error, some of the land in the vicinity of Devil's Hole (now known as the Ash Meadows National Wildlife Refuge) passed into private ownership. Within a short time wells had been sunk in the area, with the result that water levels in the subterranean aquifers (water-bearing layers of permeable rock, sand, or gravel) supplying Devil's Hole began to suffer.

By 1969, 60 percent of the Devil's Hole shelf was exposed by the drop in water level, posing a serious threat to the fish. Urgent action was taken. Specimens were transferred to several fishless desert springs, aquarium breeding projects were set up, and a fiberglass ledge with overhead lights was installed at a suitable depth within Devil's Hole itself. The last measure proved considerably more successful than the other salvage attempts. After several years of further campaigning, and a series of court hearings, the

Devil's Hole pupfish obtained its legal lifeline in 1976. The ruling set out to limit the amount of water that could be pumped from the area. The pupfish has experienced further threats since, but has managed to survive with the help of scientists and conservationists.

Conservation Measures

To check natural population levels, researchers carry out a count at least twice a year, diving 80 feet (25 m) to the shelf known as Anvil Rock. They record every fish encountered during the gradual ascent to the surface. In addition, an above-water count of fish on the shallower ledge is carried out. Depending on the time of year, counts vary from under 200 specimens to over 500. The highest numbers are recorded following the spawning season in the summer; they drop off during the winter when the algal mat dies back, largely due to lack of sunlight. A species "safety net" can be found in three specially built ponds or "refugia." Each contains subpopulations of pupfish; two of the ponds have about 200 fish, while in the third, breeding has only just begun.

As long as conditions in Devil's Hole remain within certain limits, it would seem that naturally fluctuating population levels may not adversely affect the continued survival of the species.

Glossary

Words in SMALL CAPITALS refer to other entries in the glossary.

Adaptation features of an animal that adjust it to its environment; may be produced by evolution—e.g., camouflage coloration

Adaptive radiation where a group of closely related animals (e.g., members of a FAMILY) have evolved differences from each other so that they can survive in different NICHES

Adhesive disks flattened disks on the tips of the fingers or toes of certain climbing AMPHIBIANS that enable them to cling to smooth, vertical surfaces

Adult a fully grown sexually mature animal; a bird in its final PLUMAGE

Algae primitive plants ranging from microscopic, single-celled forms to large forms, such as seaweeds, but lacking proper roots or leaves

Alpine living in mountainous areas, usually over 5,000 feet (1,500 m)

Ambient describing the conditions around an animal, e.g., the water temperature for a fish or the air temperature for a land animal

Amphibian any cold-blooded VERTEBRATE of the CLASS Amphibia, typically living on land but breathing in the water; e.g., frogs, toads, newts, salamanders

Amphibious able to live on both land and in water

Amphipod a type of CRUSTACEAN found on land and in both fresh and seawater

Anadromous fish that spend most of their life at sea but MIGRATE into fresh water for breeding, e.g., salmon

Annelid of the PHYLUM Annelida in which the body is made up of similar segments, e.g., earthworms, lugworms, leeches

Anterior the front part of an animal

Arachnid one of a group of ARTHROPODS of the CLASS Arachnida, characterized by simple eyes and four pairs of legs. Includes spiders and scorpions

Arboreal living in trees

Aristotle's lantern complex chewing apparatus of sea-urchins that includes five teeth

Arthropod the largest PHYLUM in the animal kingdom in terms of the number of SPECIES in it. Characterized by a hard, jointed EXOSKELETON and paired jointed legs. Includes INSECTS, spiders, crabs, etc.

Baleen horny substance commonly known as whalebone and growing as plates in the mouth of certain whales; used as a fringelike sieve for extracting plankton from seawater

Bill often called the beak: the jaws of a bird, consisting of two bony MANDIBLES, upper and lower, and their horny sheaths

Biodiversity the variety of SPECIES and the variation within them

Biome a major world landscape characterized by having similar plants and animals living in it, e.g., DESERT, jungle, forest

Biped any animal that walks on two legs. See QUADRUPED

Blowhole the nostril opening on the head of a whale through which it breathes

Breeding season the entire cycle of reproductive activity, from courtship, pair formation (and often establishment of territory) through nesting to independence of young

Bristle in birds a modified feather, with a bare or partly bare shaft, like a stiff hair; functions include protection, as with eyelashes of ostriches and hornbills, and touch sensors to help catch INSECTS, as with flycatchers

Brood the young hatching from a single CLUTCH of eggs

Browsing feeding on leaves of trees and shrubs

Cage bird A bird kept in captivity; in this set it usually refers to birds taken from the wild

Canine tooth a sharp stabbing tooth usually longer than the rest

Canopy continuous (closed) or broken (open) layer in forests produced by the intermingling of branches of trees

Carapace the upper part of a shell in a CHELONIAN

Carnivore meat-eating animal

Carrion rotting flesh of dead animals

Casque the raised portion on the head of certain REPTILES and birds

Catadromous fish that spend most of their life in fresh water but MIGRATE to the sea for SPAWNING, e.g., eels

Caudal fin the tail fin in fish

Cephalothorax a body region of CRUSTACEANS formed by the union of the head and THORAX. See PROSOMA

Chelicerae the first pair of appendages ("limbs") on the PROSOMA of spiders, scorpions, etc. Often equipped to inject venom

Chelonian any REPTILE of the ORDER Chelonia, including the tortoises and turtles, in which most of the body is enclosed in a bony capsule

Chrysalis the PUPA in moths and butterflies

Class a large TAXONOMIC group of related animals. MAMMALS, INSECTS, and REPTILES are all CLASSES of animals

Cloaca cavity in the pelvic region into which the alimentary canal, genital, and urinary ducts open

Cloud forest moist, high-altitude forest characterized by a dense UNDERSTORY and an abundance of ferns, mosses, and other plants growing on the trunks and branches of trees

Clutch a set of eggs laid by a female bird in a single breeding attempt

Cocoon the protective coat of many insect LARVAE before they develop into PUPAE or the silken covering secreted to protect the eggs

Colonial living together in a colony

Coniferous forest evergreen forests found in northern regions and mountainous areas, dominated by pines, spruce, and cedars

Costal riblike

Costal grooves grooves running around the body of some TERRESTRIAL salamanders; they conduct water from the ground to the upper parts of the body

Coverts small feathers covering the bases of a bird's main flight feathers on the wings and tail, providing a smooth, streamlined surface for flight

Crustacean member of a CLASS within the PHYLUM Arthropoda typified by five pairs of legs, two pairs of antennae, a joined head and THORAX, and calcerous deposits in the EXOSKELETON; e.g., crabs, shrimps, etc.

Deciduous forest dominated by trees that lose their leaves in winter (or in the dry season)

Deforestation the process of cutting down and removing trees for timber or to create open space for growing crops, grazing animals, etc.

Desert area of low rainfall typically with sparse scrub or grassland vegetation or lacking it altogether

Diatoms microscopic single-celled ALGAE

Dispersal the scattering of young animals going to live away from where they were born and brought up

Diurnal active during the day

DNA (deoxyribonucleic acid) the substance that makes up the main part of the chromosomes of all living things; contains the genetic code that is handed down from generation to generation

Domestication process of taming and breeding animals to provide help and useful products for humans

Dormancy a state in which—as a result of hormone action—growth is suspended and METABOLIC activity is reduced to a minimum

Dorsal relating to the back or spinal part of the body; usually the upper surface

Down soft, fluffy, insulating feathers with few or no shafts found after hatching on young birds and in ADULTS beneath the main feathers

Echolocation the process of perception based on reaction to the pattern of reflected sound waves (echos); occurs in bats

Ecology the study of plants and animals in relation to one another and to their surroundings

Ecosystem a whole system in which plants, animals, and their environment interact

Ectotherm animal that relies on external heat sources to raise body temperature; also known as "cold-blooded"

Edentate toothless; also any animals of the order Edentata, which includes anteaters, sloths, and armadillos

Endemic found only in one geographical area, nowhere else

Epitoke a form of marine ANNELID having particularly well developed swimming appendages

Estivation inactivity or greatly decreased activity during hot weather

Eutrophication an increase in the nutrient chemicals (nitrate, phosphate, etc.) in water, sometimes occurring naturally and sometimes caused by human activities, e.g., by the release of sewage or agricultural fertilizers

Exoskeleton a skeleton covering the outside of the body or situated in the skin, as found in some INVERTEBRATES

Explosive breeding in some AMPHIBIANS when breeding is completed over one or a very few days and nights

Extinction process of dying out at the end of which the very last individual dies, and the SPECIES is lost forever

Family a group of closely related SPECIES that often also look quite similar. Zoological FAMILY names always end in -idae. Also used to describe a social group within a SPECIES comprising parents and their offspring

Feral domestic animals that have gone wild and live independently of people

Flagship species A high-profile SPECIES, which (if present) is likely to be accompanied by many others that are typical of the habitat. (If a naval flagship is present, so is the rest of the fleet of warships and support vessels)

Fledging period the period between a young bird hatching and acquiring its first full set of feathers and being able to fly

Fledgling young bird that is capable of flight; in perching birds and some others it corresponds with the time of leaving the nest

Fluke either of the two lobes of the tail of a whale or related animal; also a type of flatworm, usually parasitic

Gamebird birds in the ORDER Galliformes (megapodes, cracids, grouse, partridges, quail, pheasants, and relatives); also used for any birds that may be legally hunted by humans

Gene the basic unit of heredity, enabling one generation to pass on characteristics to its offspring

Genus (genera, pl.) a group of closely related SPECIES

Gestation the period of pregnancy in MAMMALS, between fertilization of the egg and birth of the baby

Gill Respiratory organ that absorbs oxygen from the water. External gills occur in tadpoles. Internal gills occur in most fish

Harem a group of females living in the same territory and consorting with a single male

Hen any female bird

Herbivore an animal that eats plants (grazers and BROWSERS are herbivores)

Hermaphrodite an animal having both male and female reproductive organs

Herpetologist ZOOLOGIST who studies REPTILES and AMPHIBIANS

Hibernation becoming inactive in winter, with lowered body temperature to save energy. Hibernation takes place in a special nest or den called a hibernaculum

Homeotherm an animal that can maintain a high and constant body temperature by means of internal

processes; also called "warm-blooded"

Home range the area that an animal uses in the course of its normal activity

Hybrid offspring of two closely related SPECIES that can breed; it is sterile and so cannot produce offspring

Ichthyologist ZOOLOGIST specializing in the study of fish

Inbreeding breeding among closely related animals (e.g., cousins), leading to weakened genetic composition and reduced survival rates

Incubation the act of keeping the egg or eggs warm or the period from the laying of eggs to hatching

Indwellers ORGANISMS that live inside others, e.g., the California Bay pea crab, which lives in the tubes of some marine ANNELID worms, but do not act as PARASITES

Indigenous living naturally in a region; native (i.e., not an introduced SPECIES)

Insect any air-breathing ARTHROPOD of the CLASS Insecta, having a body divided into head, THORAX, and abdomen, three pairs of legs, and sometimes two pairs of wings

Insectivore animal that feeds on INSECTS. Also used as a group name for hedgehogs, shrews, moles, etc.

Interbreeding breeding between animals of different SPECIES, varieties, etc. within a single FAMILY or strain; Interbreeding can cause dilution of the GENE pool

Interspecific between SPECIES

Intraspecific between individuals of the same SPECIES

Invertebrates animals that have no backbone (or other bones) inside their body, e.g., mollusks, INSECTS, jellyfish, crabs

Iridescent displaying glossy colors produced (e.g., in bird PLUMAGE) not as a result of pigments but by the splitting of sunlight into light of different wavelengths; rainbows are made in the same way

Joey a young kangaroo living in its mother's pouch

Juvenile a young animal that has not yet reached breeding age

Keel a ridge along the CARAPACE of certain turtles or a ridge on the scales of some REPTILES

Keratin tough, fibrous material that forms hair, feathers, nails, and

protective plates on the skin of VERTEBRATE animals

Keystone species a SPECIES on which many other SPECIES are wholly or partially dependent

Krill PLANKTONIC shrimps

Labyrinth specialized auxiliary (extra) breathing organ found in some fish

Larva an immature form of an animal that develops into an ADULT form through METAMORPHOSIS

Lateral line system a system of pores running along a fish's body. These pores lead to nerve endings that allow a fish to sense vibrations in the water and help it locate prey, detect PREDATORS, avoid obstacles, and so on. Also found in AMPHIBIANS

Lek communal display area where male birds of some SPECIES gather to attract and mate with females

Livebearer animal that gives birth to fully developed young (usually refers to REPTILES or fish)

Mammal any animal of the CLASS Mammalia—warm-blooded VERTEBRATE having mammary glands in the female that produce milk with which it nurses its young. The class includes bats, primates, rodents, and whales

Mandible upper or lower part of a bird's beak or BILL; also the jawbone in VERTEBRATES; in INSECTS and other ARTHROPODS mandibles are mouth parts mostly used for biting and chewing

Mantle cavity a space in the body of mollusks that contains the breathing organs

Marine living in the sea

Matriarch senior female member of a social group

Metabolic rate the rate at which chemical activities occur within animals, including the exchange of gasses in respiration and the liberation of energy from food

Metamorphosis the transformation of a LARVA into an ADULT

Migration movement from one place to another and back again; usually seasonal

Molt the process in which a bird sheds its feathers and replaces them with new ones; some MAMMALS, REPTILES, and ARTHROPODS regularly molt, shedding hair, skin, or outer layers

Monotreme egg-laying MAMMAL, e.g., platypus

Montane in a mountain environment

Natural selection the process

whereby individuals with the most appropriate ADAPTATIONS are more successful than other individuals and therefore survive to produce more offspring. Natural selection is the main process driving evolution in which animals and plants are challenged by natural effects (such as predation and bad weather), resulting in survival of the fittest

Nematocyst the stinging part of animals such as jellyfish, usually found on the tentacles

Nestling a young bird still in the nest and dependent on its parents

New World the Americas

Niche part of a habitat occupied by an ORGANISM, defined in terms of all aspects of its lifestyle

Nocturnal active at night

Nomadic animals that have no fixed home, but wander continuously

Noseleaf fleshy structures around the face of bats; helps focus ULTRASOUNDS used for ECHOLOCATION

Ocelli markings on an animal's body that resemble eyes. Also, the tiny, simple eyes of some INSECTS, spiders, CRUSTACEANS, mollusks, etc.

Old World non-American continents

Olfaction sense of smell

Operculum a cover consisting of bony plates that covers the GILLS of fish

Omnivore an animal that eats a wide range of both animal and vegetable food

Order a subdivision of a CLASS of animals, consisting of a series of animal FAMILIES

Organism any member of the animal or plant kingdom; a body that has life

Ornithologist ZOOLOGIST specializing in the study of birds

Osteoderms bony plates beneath the scales of some REPTILES, particularly crocodilians

Oviparous producing eggs that hatch outside the body of the mother (in fish, REPTILES, birds, and MONOTREMES)

Parasite an animal or plant that lives on or within the body of another (the host) from which it obtains nourishment. The host is often harmed by the association

Passerine any bird of the ORDER Passeriformes; includes SONGBIRDS

Pedipalps small, paired leglike appendages immediately in front of the first pair of walking legs of spiders

97

and other ARACHNIDS. Used by males for transferring sperm to the females

Pelagic living in the upper waters of the open sea or large lakes

Pheromone scent produced by animals to enable others to find and recognize them

Photosynthesis the production of food in green plants using sunlight as an energy source and water plus carbon dioxide as raw materials

Phylum zoological term for a major grouping of animal CLASSES. The whole animal kingdom is divided into about 30 PHYLA, of which the VERTEBRATES form part of just one

Placenta the structure that links an embryo to its mother during pregnancy, allowing exchange of chemicals between them

Plankton animals and plants drifting in open water; many are minute

Plastron the lower shell of CHELONIANS

Plumage the covering of feathers on a bird's body

Plume a long feather used for display, as in a bird of paradise

Polygamous where an individual has more than one mate in one BREEDING SEASON. Monogamous animals have only a single mate

Polygynous where a male mates with several females in one BREEDING SEASON

Polyp individual ORGANISM that lives as part of a COLONY—e.g., a coral—with a saclike body opening only by the mouth that is usually surrounded by a ring of tentacles

Population a distinct group of animals of the same SPECIES or all the animals of that SPECIES

Posterior the hind end or behind another structure

Predator an animal that kills live prey

Prehensile capable of grasping

Primary forest forest that has always been forest and has not been cut down and regrown at some time

Primates a group of MAMMALS that includes monkeys, apes, and ourselves

Prosoma the joined head and THORAX of a spider, scorpion, or horseshoe crab

Pupa an INSECT in the stage of METAMORPHOSIS between a caterpillar (LARVA) and an ADULT (imago)

Quadruped any animal that walks on four legs

Range the total geographical area over which a SPECIES is distributed

Raptor bird with hooked beak and strong feet with sharp claws (talons) for seizing, killing, and dealing with prey; also known as birds of prey. The term usually refers to daytime birds of prey (eagles, hawks, falcons, and relatives) but sometimes also includes NOCTURNAL owls

Regurgitate (of a bird) to vomit partly digested food either to feed NESTLINGS or to rid itself of bones, fur, or other indigestible parts, or (in some seabirds) to scare off PREDATORS

Reptile any member of the cold-blooded CLASS Reptilia, such as crocodiles, lizards, snakes, tortoises, turtles, and tuataras; characterized by an external covering of scales or horny plates. Most are egg-layers, but some give birth to fully developed young

Roost place that a bird or bat regularly uses for sleeping

Ruminant animals that eat vegetation and later bring it back from the stomach to chew again ("chewing the cud") to assist its digestion by microbes in the stomach

Savanna open grasslands with scattered trees and low rainfall, usually in warm areas

Scapulars the feathers of a bird above its shoulders

Scent chemicals produced by animals to leave smell messages for others to find and interpret

Scrub vegetation dominated by shrubs—woody plants usually with more than one stem

Scute horny plate covering live body tissue underneath

Secondary forest trees that have been planted or grown up on cleared ground

Sedge grasslike plant

Shorebird Plovers, sandpipers, and relatives (known as waders in Britain, Australia, and some other areas)

Slash-and-burn agriculture method of farming in which the unwanted vegetation is cleared by cutting down and burning

Social behavior interactions between individuals within the same SPECIES, e.g., courtship

Songbird member of major bird group of PASSERINES

Spawning the laying and fertilizing of eggs by fish and AMPHIBIANS and some mollusks

Speciation the origin of SPECIES; the diverging of two similar ORGANISMS

through reproduction down through the generations into different forms resulting in a new SPECIES

Species a group of animals that look similar and can breed with each other to produce fertile offspring

Steppe open grassland in parts of the world where the climate is too harsh for trees to grow

Subspecies a subpopulation of a single SPECIES whose members are similar to each other but differ from the typical form for that SPECIES; often called a race

Substrate a medium to which fixed animals are attached under water, such as rocks onto which barnacles and mussels are attached, or plants are anchored in, e.g., gravel, mud, or sand in which AQUATIC plants have their roots embedded

Substratum see SUBSTRATE

Swim bladder a gas or air-filled bladder in fish; by taking in or exhaling air, the fish can alter its buoyancy

Symbiosis a close relationship between members of two SPECIES from which both partners benefit

Taxonomy the branch of biology concerned with classifying ORGANISMS into groups according to similarities in their structure, origins, or behavior. The categories, in order of increasing broadness, are: SPECIES, GENUS, FAMILY, ORDER, CLASS, PHYLUM

Terrestrial living on land

Territory defended space

Test an external covering or "shell" of an INVERTEBRATE such as a sea-urchin; it is in fact an internal skeleton just below the skin

Thorax (**thoracic**, adj.) in an INSECT the middle region of the body between the head and the abdomen. It bears the wings and three pairs of walking legs

Torpor deep sleep accompanied by lowered body temperature and reduced METABOLIC RATE

Translocation transferring members of a SPECIES from one location to another

Tundra open grassy or shrub-covered lands of the far north

Underfur fine hairs forming a dense, woolly mass close to the skin and underneath the outer coat of stiff hairs in MAMMALS

Understory the layer of shrubs,

herbs, and small trees found beneath the forest CANOPY

Ungulate one of a large group of hoofed animals such as pigs, deer, cattle, and horses; mostly HERBIVORES

Uterus womb in which embryos of MAMMALS develop

Ultrasounds sounds that are too high-pitched for humans to hear

UV-B radiation component of ultraviolet radiation from the sun that is harmful to living ORGANISMS because it breaks up DNA

Vane the bladelike main part of a typical bird feather extending from either side of its shaft (midrib)

Ventral of or relating to the front part or belly of an animal (see DORSAL)

Vertebrate animal with a backbone (e.g., fish, MAMMAL, REPTILE), usually with skeleton made of bones, but sometimes softer cartilage

Vestigial a characteristic with little or no use, but derived from one that was well developed in an ancestral form; e.g., the "parson's nose" (the fatty end portion of the tail when a fowl is cooked) is the compressed bones from the long tail of the reptilian ancestor of birds

Viviparous (of most MAMMALS and a few other VERTEBRATES) giving birth to active young rather than laying eggs

Waterfowl members of the bird FAMILY Anatidae, the swans, geese, and ducks; sometimes used to include other groups of wild AQUATIC birds

Wattle fleshy protuberance, usually near the base of a bird's BILL

Wingbar line of contrasting feathers on a bird's wing

Wing case one of the protective structures formed from the first pair of nonfunctional wings, which are used to protect the second pair of functional wings in INSECTS such as beetles

Wintering ground the area where a migrant spends time outside the BREEDING SEASON

Yolk part of the egg that contains nourishment for a growing embryo

Zooid individual animal in a colony; usually applied to corals or bryozoa (sea-mats)

Zoologist person who studies animals

Zoology the study of animals

Further Reading

Mammals

Macdonald, David, *The Encyclopedia of Mammals*, Barnes & Noble, New York, U.S., 2001

Payne, Roger, *Among Whales*, Bantam Press, U.S., 1996

Reeves, R. R., and Leatherwood, S., *The Sierra Club Handbook of Whales and Dolphins of the World*, Sierra Club, U.S., 1983

Sherrow, Victoria, and Cohen, Sandee, *Endangered Mammals of North America*, Twenty-First Century Books, U.S., 1995

Whitaker, J. O., *Audubon Society Field Guide to North American Mammals*, Alfred A. Knopf, New York, U.S., 1996

Birds

Attenborough, David, *The Life of Birds*, BBC Books, London, U.K., 1998

BirdLife International, *Threatened Birds of the World*, Lynx Edicions, Barcelona, Spain and BirdLife International, Cambridge, U.K., 2000

del Hoyo, J., Elliott, A., and Sargatal, J., eds., *Handbook of Birds of the World* Vols 1 to 6, Lynx Edicions, Barcelona, Spain, 1992–2001

Sayre, April Pulley, *Endangered Birds of North America*, Scientific American Sourcebooks, Twenty-First Century Books, U.S., 1977

Scott, Shirley L., ed., *A Field Guide to the Birds of North America*, National Geographic, U.S., 1999

Stattersfield, A., Crosby, M., Long, A., and Wege, D., eds., *Endemic Bird Areas of the World: Priorities for Biodiversity Conservation*, BirdLife International, Cambridge, U.K., 1998

Thomas, Peggy, *Bird Alert: Science of Saving*, Twenty-First Century Books, U.S., 2000

Fish

Bannister, Keith, and Campbell, Andrew, *The Encyclopedia of Aquatic Life*, Facts On File, New York, U.S., 1997

Buttfield, Helen, *The Secret Lives of Fishes*, Abrams, U.S., 2000

Reptiles and Amphibians

Corbett, Keith, *Conservation of European Reptiles and Amphibians*, Christopher Helm, London, U.K., 1989

Corton, Misty, *Leopard and Other South African Tortoises*, Carapace Press, London, U.K., 2000

Hofrichter, Robert, *Amphibians: The World of Frogs, Toads, Salamanders, and Newts*, Firefly Books, Canada, 2000

Stafford, Peter, *Snakes*, Natural History Museum, London, U.K., 2000

Insects

Borror, Donald J., and White, Richard E., *A Field Guide to Insects: America, North of Mexico*, Houghton Mifflin, New York, U.S., 1970

Pyle, Robert Michael, *National Audubon Society Field Guide to North American Butterflies*, Alfred A. Knopf, New York, U.S., 1995

General

Adams, Douglas, and Carwardine, Mark, *Last Chance to See*, Random House, London, U.K., 1992

Allaby, Michael, *The Concise Oxford Dictionary of Ecology*, Oxford University Press, Oxford, U.K., 1998

Douglas, Dougal, and others, *Atlas of Life on Earth*, Barnes & Noble, New York, U.S., 2001

National Wildlife Federation, *Endangered Species: Wild and Rare*, McGraw-Hill, U.S., 1996

Websites

http://www.abcbirds.org/ American Bird Conservancy. Articles, information about campaigns and bird conservation in the Americas

http://elib.cs.berkeley.edu/aw/ AmphibiaWeb information about amphibians and their conservation

http://animaldiversity.ummz.umich.edu/ University of Michigan Museum of Zoology animal diversity web. Search for pictures and information about animals by class, family, and common name. Includes glossary

www.beachside.org sea turtle preservation society

http://www.birdlife.net BirdLife International, an alliance of conservation organizations working in more than 100 countries to save birds and their habitats

http://www.surfbirds.com Articles, mystery photographs, news, book reviews, birding polls, and more

http://www.birds.cornell.edu/ Cornell University. Courses, news, nest-box cam

http://www.cites.org/ CITES and IUCN listings. Search for animals by scientific name of order, family, genus, species, or common name. Location by country and explanation of reasons for listings

www.ufl.edu/natsci/herpetology/crocs.htm crocodile site, including a chat room

www.darwinfoundation.org/ Charles Darwin Research Center

http://www.open.cc.uk/daptf DAPTF–Declining Amphibian Population Task Force. Providing information and data about amphibian declines. (International Director, Professor Tim Halliday, is co-author of this set)

http://www.ucmp.berkeley.edu/echinodermata the echinoderm phylum—starfish, sea-urchins, etc.

http://endangered.fws.gov information about endangered animals and plants from the U.S. Fish and Wildlife Service, the organization in charge of 94 million acres of wildlife refuges

http://forests.org/ includes forest conservation answers to queries

www.traffic.org/turtles freshwater turtles

www.iucn.org details of species, IUCN listings and IUCN publications

http://www.pbs.org/journeytoamazonia the Amazonian rain forest and its unrivaled biodiversity

http://www.audubon.org National Audubon Society, named after the ornithologist and wildlife artist John James Audubon (1785–1851). Sections on education, local Audubon societies, and bird identification

www.nccnsw.org.au site for threatened Australian species

http://cmc-ocean.org facts, figures, and quizzes about marine life

http://wwwl.nature.nps.gov/wv/ The U.S. National Park Service wildlife and plants site. Factsheets on all kinds of animals found in the parks

www.ewt.org.za endangered South African wildlife

http://www.panda.org World Wide Fund for Nature (WWF). Newsroom, press releases, government reports, campaigns. Themed photogallery

http://www.greenchannel.com/wwt/ Wildfowl and Wetlands Trust (U.K.). Founded by artist and naturalist Sir Peter Scott, the trust aims to preserve wetlands for rare waterbirds. Includes information on places to visit and threatened waterbird species

http://wdcs.org/ Whale and Dolphin Conservation Society site. News, projects, and campaigns. Sightings database

List of Animals by Group

Listed below are the common names of the animals featured in the A–Z part of this set grouped by their class, i.e., Mammals, Birds, Fish, Reptiles, Amphibians, and Insects and Invertebrates.

Bold numbers indicate the volume number and are followed by the first page number of the two-page illustrated main entry in the set.

Mammals

addax **2**:4
anoa, mountain **2**:20
anteater, giant **2**:24
antelope, Tibetan **2**:26
armadillo, giant **2**:30
ass
   African wild **2**:34
   Asiatic wild **2**:36
aye-aye **2**:42
babirusa **2**:44
baboon, gelada **2**:46
bandicoot, western barred **2**:48
banteng **2**:50
bat
   ghost **2**:56
   gray **2**:58
   greater horseshoe **2**:60
   greater mouse-eared **2**:62
   Kitti's hog-nosed **2**:64
   Morris's **2**:66
bear
   grizzly **2**:68
   polar **2**:70
   sloth **2**:72
   spectacled **2**:74
beaver, Eurasian **2**:76
bison
   American **2**:86
   European **2**:88
blackbuck **2**:94
camel, wild bactrian **3**:24
cat, Iriomote **3**:30
cheetah **3**:40
chimpanzee **3**:42
   pygmy **3**:44
chinchilla, short-tailed **3**:46
cow, Steller's sea **3**:70
cuscus, black-spotted **3**:86
deer
   Chinese water **4**:6
   Kuhl's **4**:8
   Père David's **4**:10
   Siberian musk **4**:12
desman, Russian **4**:14
dhole **4**:16
dog
   African wild **4**:22

bush **4**:24
dolphin
   Amazon river **4**:26
   Yangtze river **4**:28
dormouse
   common **4**:30
   garden **4**:32
   Japanese **4**:34
drill **4**:40
dugong **4**:46
duiker, Jentink's **4**:48
dunnart, Kangaroo Island **4**:50
echidna, long-beaked **4**:60
elephant
   African **4**:64
   Asian **4**:66
elephant-shrew, golden-rumped **4**:68
ferret, black-footed **4**:72
flying fox
   Rodrigues (Rodriguez) **4**:84
   Ryukyu **4**:86
fossa **4**:90
fox, swift **4**:92
gaur **5**:18
gazelle, dama **5**:20
gibbon, black **5**:26
giraffe, reticulated **5**:30
glider, mahogany **5**:32
gorilla
   mountain **5**:38
   western lowland **5**:40
gymnure, Hainan **5**:48
hare, hispid **5**:50
hippopotamus, pygmy **5**:52
horse, Przewalski's wild **5**:58
hutia, Jamaican **5**:64
hyena
   brown **5**:66
   spotted **5**:68
ibex, Nubian **5**:70
indri **5**:84
jaguar **5**:86
koala **6**:10
kouprey **6**:14
kudu, greater **6**:16
lemur
   hairy-eared dwarf **6**:22
   Philippine flying **6**:24
   ruffed **6**:26
leopard **6**:28
   clouded **6**:30
   snow **6**:32
lion, Asiatic **6**:34
loris, slender **6**:46
lynx, Iberian **6**:52
macaque
   barbary **6**:54
   Japanese **6**:56
manatee, Florida **6**:68
markhor **6**:72
marten, pine **6**:74
mink, European **6**:78

mole, marsupial **6**:80
mole-rat
   Balkans **6**:82
   giant **6**:84
monkey
   douc **6**:86
   Goeldi's **6**:88
   proboscis **6**:90
mouse, St. Kilda **6**:92
mulgara **6**:94
numbat **7**:14
nyala, mountain **7**:18
ocelot, Texas **7**:20
okapi **7**:22
orang-utan **7**:26
oryx
   Arabian **7**:28
   scimitar-horned **7**:30
otter
   European **7**:32
   giant **7**:34
   sea **7**:36
ox, Vu Quang **7**:44
panda
   giant **7**:48
   lesser **7**:50
pangolin, long-tailed **7**:52
panther, Florida **7**:54
pig, Visayan warty **7**:68
pika, steppe **7**:74
platypus **7**:82
porpoise, harbor **7**:86
possum, Leadbeater's **7**:88
potoroo, long-footed **7**:90
prairie dog, black-tailed **7**:92
pygmy-possum, mountain **8**:4
quagga **8**:8
rabbit
   Amami **8**:12
   volcano **8**:14
rat, black **8**:24
rhinoceros
   black **8**:26
   great Indian **8**:28
   Javan **8**:30
   Sumatran **8**:32
   white **8**:34
rock-wallaby, Prosperine **8**:36
saiga **8**:42
sea lion, Steller's **8**:62
seal
   Baikal **8**:70
   gray **8**:72
   Hawaiian monk **8**:74
   Mediterranean monk **8**:76
   northern fur **8**:78
sheep, barbary **8**:88
shrew, giant otter **8**:90
sifaka, golden-crowned **8**:92
sloth, maned **9**:6
solenodon, Cuban **9**:16
souslik, European **9**:18
squirrel, Eurasian red **9**:28

tahr, Nilgiri **9**:46
takin **9**:50
tamarin, golden lion **9**:52
tapir
   Central American **9**:56
   Malayan **9**:58
tenrec, aquatic **9**:64
thylacine **9**:66
tiger **9**:68
tree-kangaroo, Goodfellow's **10**:4
vicuña **10**:28
whale
   blue **10**:40
   fin **10**:42
   gray **10**:44
   humpback **10**:46
   killer **10**:48
   minke **10**:50
   northern right **10**:52
   sei **10**:54
   sperm **10**:56
   white **10**:58
wildcat **10**:62
wolf
   Ethiopian **10**:64
   Falkland Island **10**:66
   gray **10**:68
   maned **10**:70
   red **10**:72
wolverine **10**:74
wombat, northern hairy-nosed **10**:76
yak, wild **10**:90
zebra
   Grevy's **10**:92
   mountain **10**:94

Birds

akiapolaau **2**:6
albatross, wandering **2**:8
amazon, St. Vincent **2**:14
asity, yellow-bellied **2**:32
auk, great **2**:38
barbet, toucan **2**:54
bellbird, three-wattled **2**:82
bird of paradise, blue **2**:84
bittern, Eurasian **2**:90
blackbird, saffron-cowled **2**:92
bowerbird, Archbold's **3**:8
bustard, great **3**:10
cassowary, southern **3**:28
cockatoo, salmon-crested **3**:52
condor, California **3**:60
coot, horned **3**:62
cormorant, Galápagos **3**:64
corncrake **3**:66
courser, Jerdon's **3**:68
crane, whooping **3**:76
crow, Hawaiian **3**:82
curlew, Eskimo **3**:84
dipper, rufous-throated **4**:18

dodo **4**:20
duck
   Labrador **4**:42
   white-headed **4**:44
eagle
   harpy **4**:52
   Philippine **4**:54
   Spanish imperial **4**:56
finch
   Gouldian **4**:74
   mangrove **4**:76
firecrown, Juan Fernández **4**:78
flamingo, Andean **4**:80
flycatcher, Pacific royal **4**:82
fody, Mauritius **4**:88
grebe, Atitlán **5**:42
guan, horned **5**:44
gull, lava **5**:46
honeyeater, regent **5**:54
hornbill, writhed **5**:56
huia **5**:60
hummingbird, bee **5**:62
ibis, northern bald **5**:72
kagu **5**:88
kakapo **5**:90
kea **5**:92
kestrel
   lesser **5**:94
   Mauritius **6**:4
kite, red **6**:6
kiwi, brown **6**:8
lark, Raso **6**:18
lovebird, black-cheeked **6**:48
macaw
   hyacinth **6**:58
   Spix's **6**:60
magpie-robin, Seychelles **6**:62
malleefowl **6**:64
manakin, black-capped **6**:66
mesite, white-breasted **6**:76
murrelet, Japanese **7**:4
nene **7**:10
nuthatch, Algerian **7**:16
owl
   Blakiston's eagle **7**:38
   Madagascar red **7**:40
   spotted **7**:42
parrot, night **7**:58
peafowl, Congo **7**:60
pelican, Dalmatian **7**:62
penguin, Galápagos **7**:64
petrel, Bermuda **7**:66
pigeon
   pink **7**:70
   Victoria crowned **7**:72
pitta, Gurney's **7**:78
plover, piping **7**:84
quetzal, resplendent **8**:10
rail, Guam **8**:18
rockfowl, white-necked **8**:38
sandpiper, spoon-billed **8**:54

scrub-bird, noisy **8**:56
sea-eagle, Steller's **8**:64
siskin, red **8**:94
spatuletail, marvelous **9**:20
spoonbill, black-faced **9**:26
starling, Bali **9**:30
stilt, black **9**:32
stork, greater adjutant **9**:34
swallow, blue **9**:42
swan, trumpeter **9**:44
takahe **9**:48
tanager, seven-colored **9**:54
teal, Baikal **9**:62
tragopan, Temminck's **9**:94
turaco, Bannerman's **10**:10
vanga, helmet **10**:26
vireo, black-capped **10**:32
vulture, Cape griffon **10**:34
warbler
   aquatic **10**:36
   Kirtland's **10**:38
woodpecker
   ivory-billed **10**:78
   red-cockaded **10**:80
wren, Zapata **10**:86

Fish

anchovy, freshwater **2**:16
angelfish, masked **2**:18
archerfish, western **2**:28
barb, bandula **2**:52
caracolera, mojarra **3**:26
catfish, giant **3**:32
cavefish, Alabama **3**:34
characin, blind cave **3**:38
cichlids, Lake Victoria
   haplochromine **3**:48
cod
   Atlantic **3**:54
   trout **3**:56
coelacanth **3**:58
dace, mountain blackside **3**:90
danio, barred **3**:94
darter, watercress **4**:4
dragon fish **4**:36
eel, lesser spiny **4**:62
galaxias, swan **5**:16
goby, dwarf pygmy **5**:34
goodeid, gold sawfin **5**:36
ikan temoleh **5**:82
lungfish, Australian **6**:50
paddlefish **7**:46
paradisefish, ornate **7**:56
pirarucu **7**:76
platy, Cuatro Ciénegas **7**:80
pupfish, Devil's Hole **7**:94
rainbowfish, Lake Wanam **8**:20
rasbora, vateria flower **8**:22
rocky, eastern province **8**:40
salmon, Danube **8**:52
seahorse, Knysna **8**:68
shark
   basking **8**:80

   great white **8**:82
   silver **8**:84
   whale **8**:86
sturgeon, common **9**:36
sucker, razorback **9**:38
sunfish, spring pygmy **9**:40
toothcarp, Valencia **9**:80
totoaba **9**:92
tuna, northern bluefin **10**:8
xenopoecilus **10**:88

Reptiles

alligator
   American **2**:10
   Chinese **2**:12
boa
   Jamaican **3**:4
   Madagascar **3**:6
chameleon, south central lesser **3**:36
crocodile, American **3**:80
dragon, southeastern lined earless **4**:38
gecko, Round Island day **5**:22
gharial **5**:24
Gila monster **5**:28
iguana
   Fijian crested **5**:74
   Galápagos land **5**:76
   Galápagos marine **5**:78
   Grand Cayman blue rock **5**:80
Komodo dragon **6**:12
lizard
   blunt-nosed leopard **6**:36
   flat-tailed horned **6**:38
   Ibiza wall **6**:40
   sand **6**:42
python, woma **8**:6
racer, Antiguan **8**:16
skink, pygmy blue-tongued **9**:4
snake
   eastern indigo **9**:10
   leopard **9**:12
   San Francisco garter **9**:14
tortoise **9**:82
   Egyptian **9**:84
   Desert **9**:82
   Galápagos giant **9**:86
   geometric **9**:88
   plowshare **9**:90
tuatara **10**:6
turtle
   Alabama red-bellied **10**:12
   bog **10**:14
   Chinese three-striped box **10**:16
   hawksbill **10**:18
   pig-nosed **10**:20
   western swamp **10**:22
   yellow-blotched sawback map **10**:24
viper, Milos **10**:30
whiptail, St. Lucia **10**:60

Amphibians

axolotl **2**:40
frog
   gastric-brooding **4**:94
   green and golden bell **5**:4
   Hamilton's **5**:6
   harlequin **5**:8
   red-legged **5**:10
   tinkling **5**:12
   tomato **5**:14
mantella, golden **6**:70
newt, great crested **7**:12
olm **7**:24
salamander
   California tiger **8**:44
   Japanese giant **8**:46
   Ouachita red-backed **8**:48
   Santa Cruz long-toed **8**:50
toad
   golden **9**:70
   Mallorcan midwife **9**:72
   natterjack **9**:74
   western **9**:76
toadlet, corroboree **9**:78

Insects and Invertebrates

ant, European red wood **2**:22
beetle
   blue ground **2**:78
   hermit **2**:80
butterfly
   Apollo **3**:12
   Avalon hairstreak **3**:14
   birdwing **3**:16
   Hermes copper **3**:18
   large blue **3**:20
   large copper **3**:22
clam, giant **3**:50
crab
   California Bay pea **3**:72
   horseshoe **3**:74
crayfish, noble **3**:78
cushion star **3**:88
damselfly, southern **3**:92
earthworm, giant gippsland **4**:58
emerald, orange-spotted **4**:70
leech, medicinal **6**:20
longicorn, cerambyx **6**:44
mussel, freshwater **7**:6
nemertine, Rodrigues **7**:8
sea anemone, starlet **8**:58
sea fan, broad **8**:60
sea-urchin, edible **8**:66
snail, *Partula* **9**:8
spider
   great raft **9**:22
   Kauai cave wolf **9**:24
tarantula, red-kneed **9**:60
worm
   palolo **10**:82
   velvet **10**:84

Set Index

A **bold** number indicates the volume number and is followed by the relevant page number or numbers (e.g., **1:**52, 74).

Animals that are main entries in the A–Z part of the set are listed under their common names, alternative common names, and scientific names. Animals that appear in the data panels as Related endangered species are also listed under their common and scientific names.

Common names in **bold** (e.g., **addax**) indicate that the animal is a main entry in the set. Underlined page numbers (e.g., **2:**12) indicate the first page of the two-page main entry on that animal.

Italic volume and page references (e.g., *1:57*) indicate illustrations of animals in other parts of the set.

References to animals that are listed by the IUCN as Extinct (EX), Extinct in the Wild (EW), or Critically Endangered (CR) are found under those headings.

spp. means species.

A

Aceros spp. **5:**56
  A. leucocephalus **5:**5
Acestrura bombus **4:**78
Acinonyx jubatus **3:**40
Acipenser
  A. nudiventris **9:**36
  A. sturio **9:**36
Acrantophis madagascariensis **3:**6
Acrocephalus spp. **10:**36
  A. paludicola **10:**36
adaptation, reproductive strategies **1:**25
addax 2:4
Addax nasomaculatus **2:**4
Adelocosa anops **9:**24
Adranichthyis kruyti **10:**88
Aegialia concinna **2:**80
Aegypius monachus **10:**34
Aepypodius bruijnii **6:**64
Afropavo congensis **7:**60
Agapornis
  A. fischeri **6:**48
  A. nigrigenis **6:**48
Agelaius xanthomus **2:**92
Aglaeactis aliciae **4:**78
agricultural land use **1:**38, 61
agricultural practices **1:**52, 74; **2:**60, 63, 73, 92; **3:**10, 13, 67, 85; **4:**19, 24, 75; **5:**50, 94; **6:**6, 36, 38, 48, 82, 95; **7:**12, 19; **8:**95; **9:**4, 18; **10:**14, 34
Ailuroedus dentirostris **3:**8
Ailuropoda melanoleuca **7:**48
Ailurus fulgens **7:**50
akiapolaau 2:6
ala Balik **8:**52
Alabama **3:**34
alala **3:**82
Alauda razae **6:**18

albatross
  various **2:**9
  wandering 2:8
Algeria **7:**16
alien species **1:**71; **2:**7, 56, 77; **3:**27, 65, 83; **4:**15, 20, 50, 76, 78, 79, 88; **5:**6, 11, 17, 22, 36, 43, 46, 50, 61, 64, 74, 76, 88, 92; **6:**8, 19, 62, 65, 78, 80, 94; **7:**5, 9, 10, 14, 59, 66, 70, 82, 90; **8:**12, 19, 20, 40, 16; **9:**9, 16, 28, 32, 38, 48, 72, 81, 88; **10:**60, 87, 88
Alligator
  A. mississippiensis **2:**10
  A. sinensis **2:**12
alligator
  American 2:10
  Chinese 2:12
Allocebus trichotis **6:**22
Allotoca maculata **5:**36
Alsophis spp. **8:**16
  A. antiguae **8:**16
Alytes muletensis **9:**72
Amandava formosa **4:**74
amarillo **5:**36
amazon
  St. Vincent 2:14
  various **2:**14
Amazona spp. **2:**14
  A. guildingii **2:**14
Amblyopsis
  A. rosae **3:**34
  A. spelaea **3:**34
Amblyornis flavifrons **3:**8
Amblyrhynchus cristatus **5:**78
Ambystoma
  A. macrodactylum croceum **8:**51
  A. mexicanum **2:**40
Amdystoma spp. **8:**44
  A. californiense **8:**44
Ameca splendens **5:**36

Ammotragus lervia **8:**88
amphibians **1:**76
  diversity **1:**76
  risks **1:**78
  strategies **1:**76
  see also List of Animals by Group, page 100
Anas spp. **9:**62
  A. formosa **9:**62
  A. laysanensis **7:**10
  A. wyvilliana **7:**10
anchovy, freshwater 2:16
Andes **2:**74; **3:**46; **4:**80; **10:**28
Andrias
  A. davidianus **8:**46
  A. japonicus **8:**46
anemone *see* sea anemone
angelfish
  masked 2:18
  resplendent pygmy **2:**19
Angola **10:**94
angonoka **9:**90
animal products **1:**46; **3:**28, 75; **10:**42, 58
anoa
  lowland **2:**20; **6:**14
  mountain 2:20
Anoa mindorensis **2:**20
Anodorhynchus spp. **6:**60
  A. hyacinthus **6:**58
Anser erythropus **7:**10
ant, European red wood 2:22
anteater
  banded **7:**14
  fairy **2:**25
  giant 2:24
  marsupial **7:**14
  scaly **7:**52
antelope **2:**4, 26; 94; **4:**48; **5:**20; **6:**16; **7:** 18, 28, 30; **8:**42
Anthornis melanocephala **5:**54
Anthracoceros
  A. marchei **5:**56
  A. montani **5:**56
Antigua **8:**16
Antilope cervicapra **2:**94
Antilophia bokermanni **6:**66
aoudad **8:**88
ape, barbary **6:**54
Aplonis spp. **9:**30
Apodemus sylvaticus hirtensis **6:**92
Apteryx spp. **6:**9
  A. mantelli **6:**8
aquaculture **8:**55
aquarium trade **1:**49; **4:**36; **8:**23, 69, 84
Aquila spp. **4:**56
  A. adalberti **4:**56
Aramidopsis palteni **3:**66
arapaima **7:**76
Arapaima gigas **7:**76
archerfish
  few-scaled **2:**28
  large-scaled **2:**28

  western **2:**28
Archiboldia papuensis **3:**8
archipelagos **1:**32
  see also islands
Arctic **2:**70
Arctic Ocean **10:**58
Arctocephalus spp. **8:**62, 78
Ardeotis nigriceps **3:**10
Argentina **3:**46; 62; **4:**18
Arizona **3:**60
armadillo
  giant 2:30
  various **2:**30
arowana, Asian **4:**36
artificial fertilization **1:**88
Asia **3:**10, 66; **6:**20
asity
  Schlegel's **2:**32
  yellow-bellied 2:32
Aspidites ramsayi **8:**6
ass
  African wild 2:34; **8:**8
  Asiatic wild 2:36; **8:**8
  half- **2:**36
  Syrian wild *1:37*
Astacus astacus **3:**78
Asterina phylactica **3:**88
Astyanax mexicanus **3:**38
Atelopus varius **5:**8
Atlantic Ocean **3:**54, 88; **8:**72, 76, 80; **9:**36; **10:**8, 40, 43
Atlantisia rogersi **3:**66
Atlapetes flaviceps **4:**76
Atrichornis
  A. clamosus **8:**56
  A. rufescens **8:**56
auk, great 2:38
aurochs *1:37*
Australia **2:**16, 28, 48, 56; **3:**16, 28; **4:**38, 46, 50, 58, 74, 94; **5:**12, 32, 54; **6:**10, 51, 64, 80, 94; **7:**14, 58, 82, 88, 90; **8:**4, 6, 36, 56; **9:**4, 66, 78; **10:**20, 22, 77
Austroglanis barnardi **3:**32
avadavat, green **4:**74
avahi **5:**84; **8:**93
Avahi occidentalis **5:**84; **8:**93
Axis kuhlii **4:**8
axolotl 2:40; **8:**44
aye-aye 2:42

B

babirusa 2:44
baboon, gelada 2:46
Babyrousa babyrussa **2:**44
baiji **4:**28
Balaenoptera
  B. acutorostrata **10:**50
  B. borealis **10:**54
  B. musculus **10:**40
  B. physalus **10:**42
Balantiocheilos melanopterus **8:**84
Balantiopteryx infusca **2:**64
Balearic Islands **6:**40; **9:**72

Bali **9:**30, 68
Baltic **8:**72; **9:**36
bandicoot
  eastern barred **2:**48
  golden **2:**48
  greater rabbit-eared *1:36*
  little barred **2:**48
  Shark Bay striped **2:**48
  western barred 2:48
Bangladesh **2:**72
banteng 2:50
barb
  bandula 2:52
  seven-striped **5:**82
  various **2:**52
barbet
  toucan 2:54
  various **2:**54
Barbus (Puntius) spp. **2:**52
  B. (P.) bandula **2:**52
bat
  Australian false vampire **2:**56
  ghost 2:56
  gray 2:58
  greater horseshoe 2:60
  greater mouse-eared 2:62
  Guatemalan **2:**62
  Indiana **2:**62
  Kitti's hog-nosed 2:64
  Morris's 2:66
  mouse-tailed **2:**64
  myotis, various **2:**64
  sheath-tailed **2:**64
  see also flying fox
Bawean Island **4:**8
bear
  Asian black **2:**68
  Asiatic black **2:**74
  brown **2:**68
  grizzly 2:68
  Mexican grizzly *1:37*; **2:**68
  polar 2:70
  sloth 2:72
  spectacled **2:**74
beaver, Eurasian 2:76
beetle
  blue ground 2:78
  Ciervo scarab **2:**80
  delta green ground **2:**78
  Giuliani's dune scarab **2:**80
  hermit 2:80
  longhorn **6:**44
  scarab **2:**80
behavior studies **1:**85
bellbird
  bare-throated **2:**82
  Chatham Island **5:**54
  three-wattled 2:82
Belontia signata **7:**56
beloribitsa **8:**52
beluga **10:**58
Bering Sea **8:**62
Bermuda **7:**66
bettong, northern **7:**90
Bettongia tropica **7:**90
Bhutan **8:**28; **9:**50
big-game hunting **1:**47; **9:**68

Acknowledgments

The authors and publishers would like to thank the following people and organizations:
Aquamarines International Pvt. Ltd., Sri Lanka, especially Ananda Pathirana; Aquarist & Pond keeper Magazine, U.K.; BirdLife International (the global partnership of conservation organizations working together in over 100 countries to save birds and their habitats). Special thanks to David Capper; also to Guy Dutson and Alison Stattersfield; Sylvia Clarke (Threatened Wildlife, South Australia); Mark Cocker (writer and birder); David Curran (aquarist specializing in spiny eels, U.K.); Marydele Donnelly (IUCN sea turtle specialist); Svein Fossa (aquatic consultant, Norway); Richard Gibson (Jersey Wildlife Preservation Trust, Channel Islands); Paul Hoskisson (Liverpool John Moores University); Derek Lambert; Pat Lambert (aquarists specializing in freshwater livebearers); Lumbini Aquaria Wayamba Ltd., Sri Lanka, especially Jayantha Ramasinghe and Vibhu Perera; Isolda McGeorge (Chester Zoological Gardens); Dr. James Peron Ross (IUCN crocodile specialist); Zoological Society of London, especially Michael Palmer, Ann Sylph, and the other library staff.

Picture Credits

Abbreviations

AL   Ardea London
BBC   BBC Natural History Unit
BCC   Bruce Coleman Collection
FLPA Frank Lane Photographic Agency
NHPA Natural History Photographic Agency
OSF   Oxford Scientific Films
PEP   Planet Earth Pictures
b = bottom; **c** = center; **t** = top; **l** = left; **r** = right

Jacket

Ibiza wall lizard, illustration by Denys Ovenden from *Collins Field Guide: Reptiles and Amphibians of Britain and Europe*; Grevy's zebra, Stan Osolinski/Oxford Scientific Films; Florida panther, Lynn M. Stone/BBC Natural History Unit; silver shark, Max Gibbs/Photomax; blue whale, Tui de Roy/Oxford Scientific Films

7 C.C. Lockwood/OSF; **9** Kathie Atkinson/OSF; **11** Stephen Mills/OSF; **12–13** Roger Wilmshurst/FLPA; **14–15** A.G. (Bert) Wells/OSF; **18–19** Owen Newman/OSF; **23** Gerard Lacz/FLPA; **25** P. Morris/AL; **27** Konrad Wothe/OSF; **28–29** Mike Hill/OSF; **31** R. & M. van Nostrand/FLPA; **33** Geoff du Feu/PEP; **34–35** Gunter Ziesler/BCC; **36–37** François Gohier/AL; **39** F.W. Lane/FLPA; **43** John Cancalosi/BCC; **47** Norbert Wu/OSF; **49** Keren Su/OSF; **51** Jurgen & Christine Sohns/FLPA; **52–53** Nick Gordon/OSF; **55** Lynn M. Stone/BBC; **57** Aquarian Fish Foods; **61** Kenneth W. Fink/AL; **63** David Cayless/OSF; **64–65** D. Parer & E. Parer-Cook/AL; **65** Stan Osolinski/OSF; **68–69** Daniel Heuclin/NHPA; **71** Nick Garbutt/PEP; **73** C.B. & D.W. Frith/BCC; **75** Andrey Zvoznikov/PEP; **76–77** Max Gibbs/Photomax; **81 & 81** inset D.J. Lambert; **83** Dave Watts; **85** Tom Ulrich/OSF; **86–87** Mark Tasker/ICCE; **89 & 91** Dave Watts; **93** Mark Hamblin/OSF; **95** Karl Switak/NHPA.

Artists

Graham Allen, Norman Arlott, Priscilla Barrett, Trevor Boyer, Ad Cameron, David Dennis, Karen Hiscock, Chloe Talbot Kelly, Mick Loates, Michael Long, Malcolm McGregor, Denys Ovenden, Oxford Illustrators, John Sibbick, Joseph Tomelleri, Dick Twinney, Ian Willis